BLOWING the LID OFF the GOD-BOX

Opening Up to a Limitless Faith

Anne Robertson

morehouse

HARRISBURG • LONDON

Morehouse Publishing, P.O. Box 1321, Harrisburg, PA 17105

Morehouse Publishing, The Tower Building, 11 York Road, London SE1 7NX

Morehouse Publishing is a Continuum imprint.

Cover design by Lee Singer

Cover art by Dorothy Thompson Perez

Library of Congress Cataloging-in-Publication Data

Robertson, Anne, 1959-
  Blowing the lid off the God-box : opening up to a limitless faith / by Anne Robertson.
       p. cm.
  ISBN 0-8192-2178-3 (pbk.)
  1. God. 2. Theology. I. Title.
  BT103.R63 2005
  230—dc22
                                        2004021096

Printed in the United States of America

05 06 07 08 09 10   6 5 4 3 2 1

To **Celeste Vigneau Dyer,**
my eternal friend

**Fish don't hold the sacred liquid
in cups.
They swim in huge fluid freedom.**

—Rumi

Contents

Acknowledgments

So many people have made this book possible. It began with Jennifer Hudson, who called me to say she had dreamt of this book. The title was the title in her dream. It then continued through the generosity of those at St. John's United Methodist Church who allowed me to take all of my vacation time at once to go write it in the summer of 2001. Then there were the fine folks at Mersey River Chalets in Nova Scotia, where I hid out for a month to write. I thoroughly enjoyed my stay in cabin no. 3, my visits with Tim, Andrea, and Isabel, and the courtesy they extended in letting me use e-mail from their dining room. I was using the e-mail to send chapters home to the dedicated folks who agreed to read as I was writing: Barbara Rimes, Ken Mitchell, and my mother, Joan Thompson. I am so glad she read it then, as she has drifted into the fog of Alzheimer's and could not do so now. There were those back at St. John's who read the whole thing on my return and made comments: Nancy Johnson, Bill McWilliams, Diana Schuman, Bill and Joan Humphrey. And then there was Liz Stull, who gave it a once-over with her copyediting eye. There was Steve Swecker, the editor of *Zion's Herald*. He encouraged me, helped me put together a marketing package with which to approach editors, gave me a testimonial to go with it, and published the sermon that got me noticed at Morehouse. Cathy Brown of Expressions photography took the publicity portrait. To all those people along the way who helped me to see that God was bigger than my understanding, especially seminary professors Rod Hunter, who helped me find my voice; and Luke Timothy Johnson, who helped me believe in the voice I found ... thank you.

Prelude

Be Not Afraid

All Americans remember where they were. I was walking across the church parking lot to meet a 9 a.m. appointment, when someone drove in with the news. At first it was hard to absorb, planes hitting buildings . . . on purpose . . . terrorism . . . death. Surely it couldn't be that terrible; surely there was some explanation. As I alternated being glued to my television and scrambling to organize vigils and services at the church, I realized that yes, it was that terrible; and there was an explanation.

What happened in New York and Washington and Pennsylvania on September 11, 2001, is an extreme example of religious faith run amok, the disastrous results of confining God to a particular ideology and agenda. It was chilling enough to survey the massive death and destruction caused by the terrorist attacks, but the thing that froze the blood in my veins came a little bit later, when they released the text of the instructions to the hijackers.

> "Remind your soul to listen and obey."
>
> "Remember God frequently."
>
> "Purify your soul from all blemishes. Completely forget something called 'this life.' The time for play is over and the serious time is upon us. How much time have we wasted in our lives?"
>
> "If God gives you victory, no one can beat you. And if He betrays you, who can give you victory without Him? So the faithful put their trust in God."

I was horrified. I've taught a lot of things like that. Which of these statements couldn't be supported by the Bible? Don't Christians believe these things?

But these weren't Sunday school lessons. They were instructions for how to prepare to kill. After these expressions of piety came the guidelines for slaughtering thousands in the name of God.

I was frightened to the core. I had made similar statements from the pulpit. Had I been wrong? How? What would keep someone in my congregation from taking my words and making them a mandate for barbarity? Some thinkers have claimed that religion will always lead to atrocity. Was this proof? What would stop religious zealotry from going so far? I remembered what I'd spent the previous summer writing about: don't try to close the lid on the box of your experience with God. The metaphor of a closed God-box—denying the truth of any experience of God outside of our own—was both timely and relevant to my question.

Religion becomes atrocity, I think, in the same way that fresh water becomes a stagnant pool: when the water can't flow freely in and out. When we become closed to aspects of God that we don't understand or to experiences of God that aren't our own, we create the fiction that we know all there is to know of God and God's ways. Our limited experience and expression then become the standard by which all others are measured and the truth by which all others are judged. Inquisitions and Holocausts will follow in such a wake.

This book is an invitation to recognize our own limitations, to remember that God is God and we are not. Even as we celebrate our own particular experience of God, we must remain open to the fact that God is larger than any human experience or understanding. In the metaphor of this book, we must struggle to keep the lid off of our God-box, trusting that our understanding and experience of God are true but limited. To close the lid, to say that nothing more can be said or known about God than what we already have affirmed, is pride at its beginning and idolatry at its end. When we close the lid, very literally all hell breaks loose.

The minute we close the box on what God can be and do, we've removed God from the action and cleared the way for atrocity and violence. It's not that we start out wanting evil. We're just trying to keep God manageable: not because we're such terrible or faithless people, but because it's frightening to give up control.

The dilemma is as old as the Christian story itself, for the story of

God in a box is the story of Jesus in the tomb. The women who came to the garden on Easter morning knew that Jesus was dead. They were there at the crucifixion from beginning to end. They saw him die. They saw him taken down limp from the cross and followed as he was taken and placed in a rock-hewn tomb. When you watch someone executed and see him taken to a grave and buried, you make certain assumptions and come away with certain expectations. Foremost among those assumptions and expectations is that if you return to the grave in a couple of days, the body will still be there. It will perhaps be in a little worse shape than when you last saw it if it hasn't been embalmed, but it will still be there and it will still be quite dead.

It's a basic law of physics: bodies at rest remain at rest, and it's hard to get more at rest, at least in a physical sense, than being dead. The only concern the women had that morning was how to move the big rock that had been used to seal off the tomb. As they approached, they discovered that someone had taken care of that for them, but they still expected that the body of Jesus would be inside, and they entered to do what they'd come to do—to anoint Jesus' body with burial spices and pay their last respects.

When they got inside, however, things weren't the way they'd expected. No dead body—just an angel with the strange news that Jesus was alive and gone on ahead of them into Galilee. How did the women respond? If you'll excuse the pun, they were scared stiff. The oldest manuscripts of the Gospel of Mark end with verse 8 in chapter 16. The women discover Jesus isn't in the tomb, and they're afraid. No dancing in the streets, no celebrations of resurrection—only fear. Just when everybody thought they knew what had happened, something else throws a wrench into the works.

Now, that's not to say that the women and the other disciples weren't devastated by Jesus' death or that they wouldn't eventually be overjoyed to have him back among them. But the women's fear when Jesus isn't where he's supposed to be is typical of our response to the unexpected and the unknown. We may not like the situation in which we find ourselves, but at least if it will stay the same, we can learn how to live with it. When we know what to expect, we can plan on the stability of a routine.

But if there's one thing that was true about Jesus from the day of his birth to the day of his ascension into heaven, it was that you could expect the unexpected from him. Nobody expected the Messiah to come as a baby in a manger, born to a poor carpenter family from Nazareth. People were expecting something much more grand and impressive than that. When Jesus was twelve and seemed to be lost, his parents didn't expect to find him perfectly at home teaching in the temple. Throughout Jesus' ministry, people were surprised to see the kinds of people that he chose to associate with. They didn't understand why he broke Jewish law. The disciples didn't understand what he was doing talking with a Samaritan woman. The whole city of Jerusalem turned on him because he refused their expectations that he would be an earthly king who would overthrow the Romans.

Any Jewish scholar could tell you that the Messiah would not and could not be crucified, and even the simplest child could tell you that dead bodies sealed in tombs don't get up and go anywhere. Sure, Jesus had raised a few dead bodies, but he did it when he was alive and well himself. But now, even in death, Jesus stubbornly refused to do what all convention and protocol said he should do—to stay dead. He'd been that way in life, and death was no different.

The very thing that frightened the women—the unknown and unexpected—is that same thing that frightens us today when we consider that God might be larger and more complex than our particular experience of God. A dead God—a God sealed in a box—isn't a problem. A dead God is predictable. We can come to reverence the memory and anoint the body without having anything disrupt our plans. We can remain in control. But a *living* God—that's something else entirely. The women were afraid. So are we.

One of the primary ways we fall into sin is by trying to mold God into a God that will meet our expectations. We seek to shape God into a comfortable image and put God in a tomb-like box to examine, control, and contain. We're much more at ease when we know exactly what God thinks about every issue, when we know exactly how God will act in every circumstance, and when we can find the foolproof formula for getting into heaven and going to hell.

We're often most comfortable when we can keep our religion in the church, go there when we want to pay our respects, and be reasonably sure that God won't intrude in our day-to-day lives. We can come to the Cross, weep at the feet of Jesus, and feel righteous; but before we leave, we do want to be sure: he is *nailed* up there, isn't he? I mean he won't be getting down again, will he? I can just put this behind me and get on with my life, can't I? Most of us, if we are honest with ourselves, are very uncomfortable with a Jesus who's missing from the tomb—a God who is out of the box and roaming about unchecked.

That is, however, the central proclamation of the Christian faith: Jesus is alive. We serve a living God. A dynamic God. An unexpected God. The God of the Bible is vast beyond our comprehension. Everything that any human being can say or think about God is, at the very best, incomplete. God is too big to fit in our brain, as amazing an organ as it is. As much as we might like to, we're not going to figure God out completely. Not now, not ever.

When we serve a living Christ, we should expect to see Jesus in unexpected places and in unexpected forms. In his life on earth, Jesus was always confusing and scandalizing somebody by doing something that didn't fit in the God-box that had been built for him. He made heroes out of heretic Samaritans. He ate with sinners and tax collectors. He forgave people the Law said should be stoned to death. He openly broke Sabbath law.

Why should things be different now? Has God been tamed in the past two thousand years? What is God going to do with the souls of those young men who crashed planes into the World Trade Center, believing they were doing God's will? What is God going to do with Wiccans or Buddhists or atheists? What does God think about the gay and lesbian community?

If you're sure you know, be very careful. God may scandalize you by doing something you don't expect. God might decide to offer mercy to someone you don't think should get it. Jesus may appear in the form of someone you don't like much. God doesn't have to stay inside anybody's box—even if that box is Bible-shaped. God, who doesn't care whether you're liberal or conservative, has been known to take the sacred cows of both and turn them into gourmet burgers.[1]

There are few things more upsetting than a God who refuses to stay put—a Jesus who won't stay dead even when you seal him in the tomb and post a guard at the entrance. Jesus Christ lives and loves, eats with sinners, breaks religious law, and can no more be contained and controlled than the wind. He's not here. He is risen. He lives. So that first Easter morning the women went out and fled from the tomb, for terror and amazement had seized them.

---

1. See Bill Easum, *Sacred Cows Make Gourmet Burgers: Ministry Anytime, Anywhere, by Anyone* (Nashville: Abingdon, 1995).

To know that Jesus is alive, to know that God has blown the lid off our box, is to know that Jesus is still in the business of doing the unexpected. That doesn't have to be a frightening message. "Be not afraid," the angels were fond of saying. This is the God who loves you. God has delightful surprises in store for us, if we will allow it. In order to be truly comfortable with a living God, however, we must abandon the notion that we have God completely figured out. We've got to take our personal or denominational God-box and unseal the lid—to roll away the stone from the tomb.

Must all religion eventually lead to violence? Isn't there a way to be both faithful to the truth we affirm and open to a larger world? I believe there is, but it will take all of us, empowered by the God who broke loose from the grave. This is a book about the possibilities.

1

In the Beginning

It all began with a sermon I preached outdoors on a sunny Easter morning in Gainesville, Florida. After the sermon, the church receptionist, Jennifer Hudson, went home and had a dream. She called me at home the next day to tell me that God had told her that I needed to write a book. It was to be called *Blowing the Lid Off the God-Box*.

I can't say that God had given me the same dream, but certainly the idea—that God can't be completely contained in a box of our own making—reflected a common theme in my preaching. People were always telling me that I needed to write a book, so it seemed plausible. From that moment in 1998, I began to make notes, and the end of the story is before you.

I write in the spirit of confession, as time and experience have shown me ways I've tried to limit God's ability to work and save. I'm sure that there are still ways that I try to slam down the lid on God's freedom, but a quick review of my history will show that perhaps I've made some progress.

I had the fortune to grow up with loving parents in a Christian home. It's hard to say at what point my fairly moderate American Baptist upbringing turned to strident fundamentalism—that certainly wasn't the stance of my parents—but by the time of my baptism at age eleven, it was firmly in place. For the next ten or twelve years, I lived and breathed the cause of the Christian Right.

I handed out tracts. When the Jehovah's Witnesses came to my door, I invited them in to prove to them from the Bible that they were wrong. I lambasted our youth minister for telling the kids in the children's choir that the story of Daniel in the Lions' Den wasn't true. I was in all sorts of churches whenever the doors were open. An American Baptist on Sunday mornings, I moonlighted at an Assemblies of God church on Sunday and Wednesday nights. Tuesday nights I could be found in a Roman Catholic prayer meeting. When my father complained that I was spending all my time helping to paint the new sanctuary at Gospel Temple, I responded to him with the words of Haggai, "Is it a time for you yourselves to live in your paneled houses, while this house lies in ruins?" (Hag 1:4). It couldn't have been easy to be my parents.

When I was a student at Bucknell University, I single-handedly freed the campus of all advertisements for transcendental meditation. When posters went up, I took them down within twenty-four hours. Eventually they were put behind glass. I taped things over the glass. I spoke out in the school paper against the Equal Rights Amendment, and from the time I met her in seventh grade, through high school and beyond, I begged and pleaded and cried and agonized with my best friend, Celeste, who would not embrace the faith and who, I felt, was going straight to hell . . . do not pass go, do not collect two hundred dollars.

But during that time, I experienced three distinct moments of grace. The first was when, at age fourteen, I volunteered to preach the sermon for Youth Sunday in my home church, the North Scituate Baptist Church in North Scituate, Rhode Island. "Sermon" is a misleading term, as it was really a five-minute testimony, but nevertheless, I found myself standing in a pulpit in front of a congregation, bringing to them what I believed to be the Word of God. It was in doing so that I had the sure sense—nothing was ambivalent in those days—that this was what God wanted me to do with the rest of my life. I was called to preach.

I call that a moment of grace because, at that point in my life, I was a menace to the gospel. To call me to preach at that point was like Jesus changing Simon's name to Peter: calling the one, who was shortly to deny him, the "rock" (Matt 16:18) and promising to build his church on that firm foundation. Some rock. Some preacher. I was intolerant, religiously bigoted, and so immersed in literature about the end times that I had no use for the present. But God was still willing to give me a future beyond myself. God called me to preach.

The second moment of grace came during college. The pastor back home was retiring after many, many years in the pulpit, and my mother was on the search committee for a new pastor. She told me that one of the candidates they were considering was a woman. That moment was God's grace in the form of a two-by-four. I could hardly bear the thought of a woman pastor. It wasn't biblical, and I didn't like it. Well, that was the very first time that I realized the contradiction between my scriptural literalism and the career goal I'd listed in my high school yearbook. I was planning to be something that I condemned in someone else.

You'd think that such a confrontation would have resulted in a larger world for me but it didn't. At least not yet. The only possibility that opened up for me was the idea that I was wrong in understanding my call to preach. My family had been supportive—even my pastor had been excited about the news—but St. Paul withheld his blessing (1 Tim 2:12), and I couldn't go forward. Maybe, I reasoned, I'd been called to do other things for God instead. Maybe I was to teach in a mission field or take on some other role in the church and I had just misunderstood because I'd been preaching at the time of the call. And so I set about to work in all sorts of areas of church life, trying to find my place and my calling.

And There Was Evening and There Was Morning, the First Day

The third moment of grace came when I returned home from college. Back in my native Rhode Island, I ventured one day into a Christian bookstore on the East Side of Providence. I was the only customer in the store and the young man behind the counter engaged me in conversation. "Are you saved?" he asked.

"Yes," I answered, without missing a beat. He was obviously pleased to hear it and proceeded to ask me to share the details of exactly when and where this all had come about. "I've been saved all my life," I answered. Well, you'd have thought I had just proclaimed Satan as my Lord and Savior. The young man's countenance dropped, and he proceeded to tell me that such a statement was unbiblical and that I obviously didn't have the slightest notion of what salvation was all about. He could tell I was deluded, unsaved, and in desperate need of his wisdom. I left the store.

Although I'd been at a loss for words in the midst of the onslaught, the words began to come as I drove home. This young man in all likelihood was contemplating marriage and family at some point. Didn't he want for his children the life I'd been given? Didn't he want his children to pray before they could speak and to grow up without ever being able to consciously name a time when they didn't know that Jesus loved and cared for them? Would he insist that they abandon all he'd taught them and go live a life without God so that they could find God again in a more dramatic way? I thought not. I knew not.

I might have been willing to question my call to preach, but I couldn't imagine that God would have labeled me "unsaved" at any previous time of my life. When was I not saved? Was it in elementary school when I asked my parents to build me a chapel in the yard? Was it when I was three and sang "Jesus Loves Me" with the cherub choir? Was it before I could speak and simply listened to my mother sing "This Is My Father's World" as I went to sleep?

Okay, so it might have been in the moment that I took a wet sponge to my bedroom wallpaper (which I hated), knowing it would be ruined but telling my parents that I was just trying to clean it, or in any of a multitude of moments when I terrorized my younger brother, Rob. It's not that my childhood was sin-free, but it wasn't faith-free either. I was in a loving relationship with God, however immature that relationship might have been.

In that moment, I decided that I was saved, always had been saved, and the man at the store was off his rocker. I also opened my God-box to a bigger world: a world where I could be unbiblical and still be saved and, therefore, a world where a woman could be unbiblical and preach the word of God. God, as it turned out, was bigger than my box, and finally I'd begun to see.

Fast forward through the sudden early death of my father, the pain of infertility— thanks again, Paul, for saying that women "will be saved through childbearing" (1 Tim 2:15)—moves to Texas, Maryland, and Florida, and religious moves to the Southern Baptist and then the United Methodist denominations. Forward to the day when my husband announced he was leaving our ten-year marriage, and the day I packed up and went to seminary. I was thirty-three, dealing with a lawsuit and threat on my life by a prison inmate, and under the care of a psychiatrist for panic disorder.

I think it's fair to say that on the day I moved to Atlanta to attend the Candler School of Theology, I had nothing, except the one thing given me back on that Youth Sunday so long ago: my call to preach. Gone was any sense that I knew what the Bible meant or how God operated in the world. Gone was any notion of my own righteousness, and the term "abundant life" seemed laughable at best. When I looked in the mirror, no one looked back. I went because of the one thing I was sure of and because it seemed that if an identity were to come from anywhere, it must begin with God. So I began anew.

Genesis is absolutely right to assert that the day properly begins with night. "And there was evening and there was morning, the first day" (Gen 1:5). My new beginning wasn't a bright new dawn. It was deep night, and there were many more battles to be fought in the years ahead before I could truly feel that dawn had come. In the meantime, I began, in the dark, to forge new ideas of who God was and who I was.

The Emperor's New Clothes

Old patterns die hard, however, and my beginning attempts at newness began to look suspiciously like my old conservative agendas in liberal clothing. I'll never forget one Sunday afternoon as I helped to clean up the sanctuary in the United Methodist church in Clarkston, Georgia, where I'd found a home. I'd just encountered some incarnation of my former, Christian-Right self and was fuming as I went about my task, filled with fury over this person's intolerance. Then it hit me like a ton of bricks. I was just as judgmental in my new clothes as I'd been in the old. I was myself what I was condemning in others. Not only had I been judgmental in the past, but I was so again; it was just a different set of behaviors that I was now ready to denounce. These were some of the reasons that the word "damn" never left my lips until I went to seminary. When you have to confront your own life, sometimes it's the only word that fits.

Fast forward through graduation, through a devastating rejection by the Board of Ordained Ministry in my first attempt at ordination in Florida, to my appointment (the rejection not withstanding) to my first church in a rural Florida town whose ideology made my teenage years look liberal. Move through three successful yet costly years of ministry there, my eventual ordination, and yet another failed marriage (this one even more devastating than the last in the seven eternal months before I had it legally annulled), to a new appointment as one of three pastors in a 3,000-member congregation in Gainesville, Florida. It was there that I preached the Easter sermon that kept Jennifer up dreaming of this book, and the ideas began to form.

Forgive Me, Father, for I Have Sinned

This book is my confession, but by that I do not mean that it is an exposé of all my various sins. It is more a confession of the sins I committed "in faith," if that much paradox doesn't make you reel. I ran across a T. S. Eliot poem that seemed to sum up my dilemma. Called "Little Gidding," it laments the hurtful things, "which once you took for exercise of virtue."

That was exactly what had happened to me: The things that I once "took for exercise of virtue" I'd now come to identify as sin. There were harmful things I'd done, but at the time, I thought they represented the unerring will of God. The biblical word for the shape this has taken in my life is "idolatry."

Both in my conservative and liberal incarnations, I broke the second commandment, which reads: "You shall not make for yourself an idol, whether in the form of anything that is in heaven above, or that is on the earth beneath, or that is in the water under the earth" (Exod 20:4). I gave dominion over my life to things other than God. In my case, the idols were made from sacred substances. I didn't idolize money or TV or a celebrity (except maybe for a brief imaginary dalliance with Donny Osmond as a young teen). Since I was steeped in faith, my idols were the things of faith—the Bible, certain practices of worship, certain doctrines—and they were all the more insidious because they bore the mark of God.

We make an idol, I believe, whenever we give something that is not God the central place that only God deserves, or when we confuse something created with the Creator. Sacred and holy things often become idols in our lives, which is one of the reasons they are so dangerous. They are much harder to see than secular idols, and the more we're bent on sharing our God with the world, the more we spread our idolatry.

In the pages that follow, I'll explore what idolatry looks like in some of these more disguised forms. But to see how it works in general, here's a simple example. Remember the saying, "Cleanliness is next to godliness"? I would bet we've all met people who have left out the "next to" part of that phrase. If your house is a mess, such people will call your salvation into question. Cleanliness is certainly a good thing, and there's nothing wrong with giving it an honored place "next to" godliness. But when we come to think that cleanliness *is* godliness, however, we've crossed the line into idolatry. If cleanliness has become your idol, it becomes the lens through which you see life and the rule by which you judge all action and behavior.

We make idols of work, family, friends, pastors, the Bible, political platforms, and many other very good things. These are all good and helpful pieces of our lives. In deposing them as idols, I don't mean to throw them out or to say they're bad in themselves. But when I ascribe to those things attributes that only God possesses, I've created an idol and fallen into sin.

In talking about such things in this book, I've used the metaphor of a God-box. The box itself isn't an idol. The box is the image we have of who God is and how we relate to God, constructed and filled over the years of our religious experience. While having the box is useful, good, and necessary, *closing* the box and trying to limit God's freedom to work in ways that are beyond our understanding and experience is what constitutes idolatry. More about that as we go along.

Of course those who worship idols don't call them closed boxes or idols. They call them "God." Obviously I don't begin this discussion with a clean slate. Before writing page one, I made the judgment that there is a God, that this God is knowable at some level and unfathomable at another, and that the nature of this God is truly revealed in the person of Jesus. I don't think that God is revealed *only* in Jesus, but I am a minister of the Christian gospel because I do believe that God is most *clearly and completely* revealed in Jesus. That's not to say that God can be completely known, even so. I'd be appalled to think that God would be so small as to be comprehensible by my limited mind. But it is to say that I believe the Christian witness has benefits that others cannot offer, and I write primarily to those who share that orientation.

This is the spirit in which I present this book. It is confession, which, as with all Christian confession, brings with it the hopeful message of grace. I shudder to think of the harm I've inflicted on others—harm that I once "took for exercise of virtue." I self-righteously thought I had a corner on who was saved and who wasn't, both from a liberal and a conservative vantage point. I thought I knew the "right" way to interpret Scripture and was quick to condemn those who thought otherwise. Nevertheless, God called me to preach. Pure grace.

In writing this, I hope to avoid merely creating another rule of judgment, although whether I succeed is for others to decide. It's a hard line to walk, as I don't believe that we can go through life with integrity if we make no judgments at all. Obviously, in writing this, I've already made distinctions between "right" and "wrong." Thank God that American society came to the judgment that slavery was wrong. Thankfully the world, for the most part, has come to judge the Holocaust as wrong, and you will see in the ensuing chapters that words like "atrocity" have substantive meaning for me. I do not think morality is relative.

But I also find that in the Kingdom of God, the naming of sin (judgment) is not the same as condemnation. In the spirit of confession, naming and facing our sins—personal or corporate, blatant or subtle—is the substance of our gospel. We judge our sins to be wrong, even horrific, in the eyes of God, and we are correct. And yet God saves us. The one whom we have crucified stands ready and willing to forgive our sin and to share with us the Kingdom of God. This is why confession is an act of hope, and judgment—the naming of sin—is the necessary predicate of grace. It is why we had to have law before we could have gospel, Good Friday before Easter.

In the name of Jesus Christ you are forgiven.
Glory to God! Amen.

2

So What's a God-Box?

This is a book about boxes. Specifically, it's a book about the types of boxes we use to try to contain God. We all have them, and in some sense we all need them, since Scripture tells us again and again that we can't stand in the full, unbounded presence of God and live. I don't think those statements represent God's desire to keep us distant or to do us harm. I think we can't stand in God's full presence for the same reason we can't look directly into the sun or hope to get a cup of water by holding a glass under the fullness of Niagara Falls.

While we dwell in our mortal state, we can only deal with the enormity and power of God by getting to know little pieces at a time. Our God-box is the way we can approach God and the means by which we can talk meaningfully about "knowing" God. It's made up of our experiences of God and our beliefs about who God is and how God behaves. It's like the data collected by scientists when they study something. They observe, they make notes, they create theories to explain what they see, and then they live with those theories to see if anything pokes a hole in them. Our God-box represents the data and theories we have collected about God. In religious terms it is our "theology."

The trap we often fall into with our God-boxes is in mistaking a piece for the whole, or in thinking that God's presence in our box precludes God's presence in any other box or even outside of boxes altogether. Once we've fallen into the trap, our God-box can become the way that we avoid dealing with the parts of God that make us uncomfortable and the way that we keep ourselves and our religious communities free of others who aren't like us. At its worst, it becomes an idol, a dead substitute for the living God.

Most of this book will describe some of the more common ways that God-boxes are misunderstood or abused, but I want to be careful not to condemn the box itself. If God were only unknowable mystery, we'd have something very different from Christian faith. It is, in fact, part of the Christian gospel to say that God will actually come and inhabit our box. Whether it was the glory of God descending on the tabernacle in the wilderness or the Word becoming flesh in Jesus Christ, there is strong biblical evidence that God will accept the limitations of the boxes we create.

Boxes are necessary, just as we need special equipment to view a solar eclipse. Besides, if I condemned boxes completely, I'd have created a box for God that confines God to not being confined. Back to Logic 101 for me. The box itself is, I think, indispensable as long as we dwell in mortal bodies. As Paul says in 1 Corinthians 13:12, the situation will change beyond the veil: "Then I will know fully, even as I have been fully known." The tricky part is staying humble enough to recognize that currently we see only as through a dim and dark glass. We must always be open to the correction of a better view.

This Side Up

To be open to correction and improvement means, in terms of the metaphor, that we should not put a lid on our God-box. It doesn't matter whether the box is our personal God-box or the God-box established by a certain community. We lose humility the minute we close it up and say, "There. Now I know all about God. I know exactly what God will and won't do, where God can and can't be, and who God will and will not accept. End of discussion." God is very good at blowing the lid off of God-boxes, and the more you have invested in the perfection of your own, the more you stand to lose when the whirlwind of God blows in and tears it to shreds.

Keeping the lid off our boxes will also make our lives in our faith communities more tolerable. While I've only been a pastor for ten years, I've been active in the church since I actively screamed as an infant in the church nursery. Across many denominations and from many viewpoints, I watched people move from church to church and, more recently, from religion to religion, in search of the "right" one. What are they looking for? In many cases, they're searching for the God-box that's perfect and complete: the place that has God completely figured out. Wonder of wonders—they don't find it. They find plenty of places that have put lids on their boxes and claim to have it all figured out, but when they look inside, they find that the contents of this God-box don't quite match their own experience of God. So they reject the entire box and move on.

Perhaps if all sides realized that there's always more to be learned, and that any time we try to reduce the vast mystery of God to human words and formulas, we never get it quite right; we could settle down and learn from one another rather than aimlessly wandering in the wilderness with no real place to call home.

When I think of the need for an open box, I think of my first trip to the Grand Canyon. I was a teenager traveling cross-country with my family. We'd seen a lot of canyons already, and it took quite a bit of coaxing for my parents to get me out of the car even to look. What was one more canyon? But I finally got out, because this was the Grand Canyon, the mother of them all, which, in all the postcards and pictures, goes on forever and ever without a glimpse of the other side. I got out. I looked. And I could see, plain as day, the other side. I could see the boundary and could tell what was canyon and what was not. Okay, so it was really big. I couldn't jump it. But I wanted more than big. I wanted unfathomable—without beginning and without end. That's what the pictures had led me to believe, and when I saw the reality, I was disappointed.

What I wanted from the Grand Canyon is available to us in God. Something without beginning and without end, something without boundaries, something infinitely bigger than me. Isn't that why people rush to the ocean when there's a big storm? Isn't that part of the thrill of storm chasing, or visiting Niagara Falls, the Rockies, or outer space? It is for me. It's also why I'm thrilled every time I read the book of Job and Yahweh finally answers Job out of the whirlwind (chapters 38–39), reminding Job of the vast gulf between God's wisdom and Job's understanding.

As much as I, like Job, might want an answer to my questions, there's a mysterious sort of comfort in knowing that there are some things beyond my knowing, that there are powers that won't even notice my puny attempts to control them. I like to control and set boundaries as much as the next person. But, in the end, I want to know that there's something bigger. I want to know that God is there: wider than the sea, stronger than the mountains, smarter than Einstein, more powerful than a Category 5 hurricane.

I remember once feeling stifled, oppressed, and controlled by a supervisor. I felt that my work was always being undermined or sabotaged, and what once had been a joy had become a nightmare. During vacation that year, I took a ferry ride. The water was stormy, but it was the only way across, so I went. For a couple of hours the ferry lurched from side to side. As I looked out the window, I could see first all water and then all sky—water, sky, water, sky—as we rocked over to one side and then back up the other.

Some people were terrified, and I suppose if I had any sense I would've been also. But instead, I felt a strange sense of comfort. As I looked out at the raging sea that was tossing this huge ferry from side to side, I realized that it could swallow my boss in an instant. At the time, that thought alone was comforting. But it also put my problems in perspective. The man who seemed to hold sway over my life would be, in the face of the power of God's ocean, unable even to save himself. The ocean isn't God; the ocean is only a creation of God, something that contained only a tiny portion of God's power.

That ferry ride gave me a better sense of who's really in charge. Thinking of my boss being swept away by the waves (after the initial flush of satisfaction) eventually gave me more compassion for him and the futility of his efforts to control me or anyone. He was my supervisor, but he was not my God. He had some derivative control, but in all things that really mattered, he could do nothing. When I went back, the situation hadn't changed, but my attitude had.

What I'm talking about is reflected in the words from the wonderful hymn "This Is My Father's World."[2] In the third verse we sing, "This is my Father's world. O, let me ne'er forget that though the wrong seems oft so strong, God is the Ruler yet." Until we've been willing to acknowledge that God is able to transcend our boxes, that God is bigger than our comprehension, we're denied the comfort of that verse and of my ferry experience. We have to let God out of the box.

But that doesn't mean we have to throw the boxes away. As long as our boxes serve rather than determine our experiences of God, they can be a helpful and delightful tool. I need to know that God is bigger and more powerful than even the greatest evils of our world. But I also need to know that God will consent to stop being a consuming fire for

---

2. Hymn #144 in *The United Methodist Hymnal* (Nashville, TN: The United Methodist Publishing House, 1989). Words by Malthie D. Babcock, 1901.

a minute and speak to me from an approachable burning bush. And it's crucial to my faith that the God who fixed the stars in place and created Leviathan would consent to be confined to a manger in Bethlehem, a tabernacle in the wilderness, or the little chapel I have in my spare bedroom. The important thing to remember is that God is contained only at God's discretion, not at our command.

Partial Shipment

Organized religion has fallen into disfavor these days, and for some very good reasons. I'm completely sympathetic when someone tells me of the hurts they've suffered at the hands of the church and lists the reasons they disavow a group that across the ages has committed atrocities in the name of Christ. I've often said that the very existence of the church today is proof of the existence of a loving and forgiving God, since by all rights we should have been obliterated long ago.

That said, however, I believe we're causing ourselves still greater harm when we shun all organized communities of faith. There are things in other people's boxes that can enrich our own. God seems to have designed the world with a myriad of plots to bring us together in community, and sending us each only a partial shipment in our God-boxes is one of them. Yes, you can worship God by yourself in the woods. I do that frequently. But if, when you open your personal God-box, you find anything to do with love inside, you'll need to find a faith community. We can't love by ourselves. In the Christian faith, it takes at least three: God, neighbor, and self.

Community is one way of being sure that our God-box stays open and useful as a tool for our spiritual growth. I have a good friend named Barbara who grew up in a hateful environment. With a harsh and demanding mother and an alcoholic, irrational father, she knew little of real love. When Barbara looked through the glass Paul mentions in 1 Corinthians 13 to try to see God, her view was not just dark but distorted. The glass was broken and painted black in many places. Her God-box, accordingly, proclaimed a God of harshness and judgment and irrational behavior.

Because of the nature of her God-box, she didn't look in it very often. She covered the box with the lid of the church, in the hopes of keeping a cruel God placated and contained. She didn't necessarily think that she'd learned everything about God, but she was afraid of what else there might be. Any more bad news and she might end up taking her life as her father had done. Better to close the box and try to follow the rules so that God wouldn't be tempted to reach out of the box and destroy her.

It took many years, but as my friend began to truly interact with others in the church, she saw new things. Other people didn't seem to be afraid of their God-boxes as she was afraid of hers. They had them open all the time and delighted in sharing the contents with one another. The more they shared, the more their boxes grew and she could swear that some actually glowed with the splendor of what was inside.

The one ingredient that seemed to be common to all of those glowing boxes was love. She talked to someone about it and bravely allowed a new friend to put just a little love into her own fear-laden box. It blew the box apart. Gone was the lid, gone were the walls, gone were all the hateful contents, leaving only that little bit of love scampering around like a puppy who had escaped its leash and was frolicking in a new world.

Together with new friends, she began the task of constructing a new and better God-box. Unlike her old box, this was one that could serve her rather than control her. With this box, she could get close to God and actually have a relationship, and her box grew and eventually began to glow like those around her.

This is what a faith community can do for us. As we interact with others who are also on a faith journey, we begin to learn that God is bigger than we are and that God uses an infinite array of objects, people, and methods to get our attention. I used to assume, for instance, that God could only speak out in the country, because that was how God spoke to me. I put that in my God-box and closed the lid. Then I met someone who found God in the bustle and steel of the city, and I discovered that my lid was premature. I grew up Baptist with a heavy dose of Assemblies of God. God was to be found, I thought, in freedom of expression and free-form worship. I put it in the box and closed the lid. Then I met a man who reveled and glowed in liturgy and ritual, and I had to take the lid off again.

I wish I could say that I never put a lid on my box these days, but that would be a lie. However, I'm better at keeping it off than I used to be, and tend to open the box back up more willingly than I did when I was younger. There are now all sorts of things in my God-box. Some have been there from childhood and some are as new as yesterday.

There are things that are distinctively Christian, like the Trinitarian God, and things that sound more Native American or New Age, like animal totems and auras. There are things that I have thrown out (like a literal view of every verse of Scripture), things that have undergone huge shifts in interpretation (like concepts of hell and damnation), and things that have grown in importance with every passing year (like "God is love," 1 John 4:8). I am sure that some things in my current box will be tossed out or changed in time and that other things will be added, but if it weren't for the sharing in the boxes of others, I wouldn't have a box that brings me such delight.

Handle with Care

Now, I can already hear someone objecting that there are unhealthy communities as well as healthy ones. There was the community of David Koresh in Waco, Texas, of Jim Jones in Guyana, of Neo-Nazi organizations, terrorist groups like Al-Qaeda, and other hate groups too numerous to mention. My own experience has been that harmful communities are those that have sealed tight the lid on their God-boxes and have encouraged me to do the same. Those who claim to know boundaries of God's love, who are certain of how God will behave in every instance, who refuse the claims that God can speak in languages outside of their experience—those communities I keep at arm's length. At their most innocent, such communities stifle the joy and freedom of a larger vision of God. At their worst, their God-box becomes an idol that eventually demands human sacrifice. The difference between healthy and harmful communities is, I think, the difference between saying "God is in this box" and saying "God is in this box only."

I've never been harmed and have often been enriched by sharing experiences with those who have an open box. It doesn't matter if they're Christian, Buddhist, Muslim, Wiccan, Pagan, something else, or nothing in particular. If both of our boxes are open, we can share without defensiveness. The difficulties in evangelism have come, I think, because of closed boxes. When we evangelize with a closed box, we do harm. Why? Because we insist that someone else's box must be identical to ours: it's our way or the highway. We demand that others serve the box rather than allowing the box to serve them.

When Native Americans said that drums were a crucial part of their God-boxes, we European-Americans refused to honor or learn from that. Because our box was closed and didn't include drums, their box was unacceptable. There was no sharing, only the imposition of a foreign box on those who couldn't relate to the experiences that were within it. Christian evangelism has done this in many times and places, and it has come back more than once to bite us.

It's God's Box After All

Before going farther, one thing has to be said. We do not construct and fill our God-boxes on our own. Various communities with which we associate have a part, but more importantly, we have the help of God. It is God who helps to direct us toward helpful communities and away from destructive ones. It is God who produces fruit in our lives when our box is filled with elements of truth, and it is God who helps us see through things we've put in our box that have no real substance.

If we were simply left to our own devices, our boxes all would be relative. There would be no lid, but perhaps there would be no bottom either, and ideas would simply flow in and out, maybe with a passing interest, but there'd be nothing that could really transform our lives. This was the case with the people of Athens when Paul took the gospel to them. Their boxes were certainly open, but they were open at both ends. God provided for them to hear the message, and they listened with interest, but it flowed right through and by morning they were ready for the next new idea.

The bottom of the box represents our willingness to let God be at work in our box. All through the Bible, God seems to ask whether the people are willing to accept God's rule. They are, to all appearances, free to say "yes," or "no." When we say "yes" to God, even though we might have only a vague idea of who that God is or what that means, we have invited God to undergird our box; with that support in place, we can begin to place things in it without fear.

Having God as the foundation to the box isn't a guarantee that we won't ever put something in the box that doesn't belong there. It does make way for God to agitate the contents when things don't flow together as they should, to blow the lid off when we've forgotten our humility, or even to blow up the box entirely if it's filled with fundamental error. Putting God in charge of our God-box is a way of acknowledging that there are absolutes in the world and that there exists unshakable truth without the arrogance of assuming that we can be certain of what that is.

It's also the way that we can live without fear. Time after time people have come into my office afraid to make a decision. It's not that they don't have preferences or inclinations, but they're paralyzed by the fear of making a wrong choice that doesn't reflect God's will for their lives. Putting God in control of our God-box is an act of faith that dispenses with such fears. Yes, you might put something wrong in the box. I've done that many times, and probably there are some clunkers in there now. But because God is the foundation, a wrong choice is not forever. God will either refine it, transform it, or keep agitating it enough that you will eventually take it out simply to keep the peace.

This is faith. It is trusting that, as Psalm 139:7–10 attests, we can't go where God cannot come:

> Where can I go from your spirit? Or where can I flee from your presence? If I ascend to heaven, you are there; if I make my bed in Sheol, you are there. If I take the wings of the morning and settle at the farthest limits of the sea, even there your hand shall lead me, and your right hand shall hold me fast.

When we put God in control of the box, it doesn't mean we won't make bad choices. It simply means that we can't make a choice that God can't use for the glory of God's kingdom. It might make our own lives difficult for a time, and we might truly suffer as a result, but in the long run even death on a cross can be used to save the world, when it is given into the hands of God.

3

In the Image of God

Some of the very first things that go into our God-boxes are images of God, and they come from all sorts of people and places. They come from our family, our friends, our church, and the environment in which we live. They begin to form the minute that we first hear the word "God," as we try to make associations that will help us understand what this new word means.

For some, the process gets derailed when they begin to read Scripture and hear the second commandment, usually ingrained as it is in the King James: "Thou shalt not make unto thee any graven image." No images, it says, and yet the Bible then goes on to give us all sorts of images by which we might imagine the Unimaginable. But perhaps there is something to be learned in the second commandment. After all, it technically doesn't say "no images," but rather no "graven image." The noun is in the singular, and the adjective describes something carved into a fixed substance.

While there are many other ways to talk about that commandment, I think part of the meaning is that we shouldn't make one "graven" image, an image that is engraved so that it cannot be reinterpreted or reconfigured, an image carved in a fixed material so that it can only be this and no other. To engrave an image of God implies a God confined and limited according to human craft and design. In the metaphor of the God-box, I think engraving an image is like closing the lid.

We need the images in order to approach God, just like we need the box. What we must be careful not to do is to engrave the God we imagine in stone, to close the lid on the box so that we begin to think that our image contains the entirety of God. That, I believe, is idolatry.

Father

Since the Lord's Prayer is often one of the first things we commit to memory as Christians, the image of "Father" is often the first thing in our God-box. "Father" works for me as an image of God because my own father was loving and good. It went in my box early, and it has remained there. It apparently also worked for Jesus (which I believe is at least partly a testament to Joseph) and it works for many others. I disagree strongly with those who would abolish "Father" from the list of appropriate images for God.

I appreciate, however, that, for many, associations with earthly fathers have so clouded the term that calling God "Father" does more harm than good. I can understand that they have no desire to put the image of "Father" into their God-box, and I'm not about to demand that they do so. But I'd still object if they closed the lid and put "Father" into exile forever. Why? Because the more terms and images we can grow to use for God, the more complete our understanding of God's nature will be. We might not be able to rule a term "in" for ourselves, but we shouldn't rule it "out" for others, or even for ourselves at another time.

There may be one day when a person has been able to process a hurtful past enough that they begin to desire and search for the father they should have had. If their God-box is still open to the possibility of God as Father, they'll recognize the fatherly love of God when it comes to them. The brokenness of the past then has a chance to be healed, and their experience of God is broadened.

Mother

Having said all of that, however, if we close our box with only the one image of "Father" in it, we're also doing ourselves a disservice because our view of God will be severely limited. It's always been a mystery to me that most people are so open to God as a father and so completely closed to God as a mother. Any father can tell you that when you compare the attention given on Father's Day and Mother's Day, the mothers win out. I read somewhere that Mother's Day sees the greatest volume of phone calls, while Father's Day sees the greatest number of collect phone calls. There are many more adult children who call their mothers every week or even every day who only talk to Dad if Mom hands him the phone. When I was growing up in the early 1960s, one of the greatest insults was to make disparaging remarks about another child's mother.

There are abusive and difficult mothers, just as there are abusive and difficult fathers, but overall in our culture, it seems to be Mom who gets the attention. So what gives with the problems of calling God "Mother"? I don't get it. I remember reading someone in seminary (my apologies to an unremembered source) who noted that we have no problem with God being animal, vegetable, or mineral but let God be imaged as a woman and cries of heresy go up from every corner. Lion of Judah, Lamb of God, the Vine, the Rock—all slide through with relative ease, even though non-Christian cultures across the globe have worshiped animals, plants, and stones. But the charge of heresy only seems to surface when we use the female image. For all the charges of patriarchy leveled at the Roman Catholic Church, at least they allow for reverence of the Mother of God.

Well-known author and preacher Barbara Brown Taylor talks about visiting the Holy Land and coming to the place where tradition says that Jesus looked down over Jerusalem and lamented, "Jerusalem, Jerusalem, the city that kills the prophets and stones those who are sent to it! How often have I desired to gather your children together as a hen gathers her brood under her wings, and you were not willing!" (Matt 23:37) What does the little chapel at the site prominently display? A rooster! They just couldn't bear to put up a female image, even in chicken form! So what's our problem? It's okay for God to be imagined as a chicken but not a woman?

For me, being able to use a female image for God is only partly an issue of social justice. That piece tends to get the most attention, so I want to start somewhere else. I think the feminine image of God is important because it enables me to know God better and to live my life more fully. I remember when it finally hit me that I could envision God as "Mother." As I was thinking through all the ins and outs of gender issues as they relate to faith, it suddenly occurred to me that using the image "Father" exclusively might be the root of many of the problems I had in relating to God.

For me, one of the last of the baby boom generation, fathers were the ones who fixed things. It's a stereotype, I know, but it formed me nonetheless. They provided solutions, whether it was answering an objective question or repairing a problem bicycle. To this day, I remember how frustrated I was when I came to my father (the history teacher) and asked him who Charlemagne was. His answer was to make me read an entire book on Charlemagne. I read the book, but it was really more than I wanted to know. I wasn't prepared to give a dead king that much time. I didn't come to him for a task. I came to him for an answer.

When I was bullied on the school bus, I reported that to my father, because he was also protector and provider. He answered questions and he fixed what was broken. While I know that wasn't true in every family, it was true in enough families that it became the stereotype. Sitcoms have proclaimed that for years. When I said that to a man in my congregation, he responded that in recent years sitcoms have also portrayed fathers "largely as bumbling idiots who can't think their way out of their own chairs. Lots of teenage kids will think of God as the Great Insensitive Screwup if they think of him exclusively in TV-father terms." Good point.

Mothers have had their traditional role, too. But it was a different role, at least in my eyes. A broken toy goes to Dad. But a broken spirit goes to Mom. I went to my father when I wanted a specific answer. I went to my mother when I wanted understanding. When a child scrapes her knee and asks Mom to "kiss it and make it better," the child does not expect the scrape to vanish into thin air. She expects comfort. I would complain to my father, "He hit me," if what I wanted was for him to go do something about it. If I said the same thing to my mother, I would have been asking for reassurance that I was so precious that no one should ever hit me. I, at least, had very different expectations from father and mother even in the same situation.

As I thought about that, I realized that much of my frustration with God came because I had never learned about God as a mother. That meant that every problem ended up going to "Dad," with all of the learned expectations that brought. Let's say I got sick. The minute I pray, "Father, I'm sick," my brain kicks in the parameters for what fathers do about things. They fix them. So when I take my illness to God as a father, I expect him to heal me then and there. To fix it. If God, my Father, doesn't fix it, I get frustrated and think that God either isn't loving or isn't really so capable after all.

How different it might be if I also had the concept of God as Mother who might not heal me on the spot, but who might hold me in her lap, put a cold cloth on my forehead, and tenderly give me comfort. Perhaps I wouldn't be frustrated with God so much of the time, if my expectations weren't always for the response of a father—to provide, to protect, to fix—but for a mother—to understand, to listen, to comfort, to validate, to nurture.

I realize not everyone carries such stereotypes around and that the women's movement has helped to free us from the stereotypes that remain. But I believe there are enough of us with at least some of those notions embedded in our brains that we need both father and mother images for God to give us balance. After all, if I look to "Dad" to fix the problem and receive "Mom's" nurture instead, I might not even recognize that God has answered my prayers.

Of course the social justice piece is also present, and I don't mean to minimize it. We need to take a long, hard look at why it's okay for God to be a rock and not a woman. Is our form truly so heinous that God would shun it? When we discover that the Bible portrays divine Wisdom as a woman and we finally realize that our gender can also be portrayed as "holy" and even "divine," do we really become heretics?

If you close the lid on female images of God, look out. At some point, God will blow the lid off. My first church was a small congregation in rural, conservative, Dixie County, Florida. They thought they had that lid nailed on tight. And God sent them me: a divorced Yankee woman pastor from a liberal seminary. We both figured God must have a warped sense of humor, but both of our boxes are now missing lids!

Partner

Even if you have been broad-minded enough to put a female image in your box, I still don't recommend closing the lid. The image of God as a loving parent of either sex is an excellent one that will carry you through a lot of situations—but not all of them. If God is always a parent, then we're always children, but sometimes we need an image of God in which we're grown-ups. God as friend or God as lover are both strong biblical images that allow us to transcend childhood and see ourselves in intimate partnership with God.

Most often our parent images are applied to God the Creator, the first person of the Trinity, while the images of friend or lover tend to drift toward Jesus. The hymn "What a Friend We Have in Jesus" can be heard in all parts of the globe, and it is Jesus we most often call "lover of my soul." But certainly those images didn't begin with Jesus. The friendship between God and Abraham amazes me every time I read about it, and if you're not aware of the image of God as Israel's husband and lover, then you've missed reading enormous chunks of Scripture.

We Protestants are especially good at the friend and lover images, but they have their drawbacks when we rely on them exclusively. We can end up becoming so buddy-buddy with God that it becomes easier to tell God to go jump in a lake when God suggests we do something or accept something that isn't to our liking. Taking our cues from Abraham, we argue with God about the justice of God's actions and try to negotiate a better deal. That isn't always appropriate. But what a gift it is to know that God's love is as mature and intimate as our closest friend and as all-consuming as the flame of lovers.

Lord

We've also missed large chunks of Scripture if we've missed the image of God as Lord, King, Ruler, Sovereign, Master, Judge, and, of course, the Creator with sole rights over the created. These are the images that help to restore humility and encourage obedience. God is God and we are not. We forget that at our peril. As with father images, these terms may be tainted by some human beings who have held those titles. I understand the concerns about domination and oppression and the worries that in an increasingly democratic world, words like "King" and "Lord" may seem meaningless. But our faith and our relationship with God are diminished if we close our box to such words.

These are the images that keep us humble. If we use them exclusively, God can become unapproachable, distant, and perhaps oppressive and unconcerned with our "plebeian" affairs. But if you put them in the box with all the others and shake them all up together, they tend to balance out our spiritual growth, moving us toward both obedience and gratitude.

Servant

Images of God as lord and king are balanced by the images of God, especially in Jesus, as shepherd, suppliant, and servant. The Hebrew Scriptures refer to earthly kings as "shepherds," showing how God intends for human authority to be used. The image of God as servant can be tricky, too. It may be dangerously easy to move from the image of Jesus washing the feet of the disciples to the thought that God, as a good servant, should do as we say. That fallacy may be much harder to fall into if we also have the images of "Lord," "Master," or "King" in our box. Our God-box should be designed like our government—full of checks and balances.

The Created Order

Finally, there are those "animal, vegetable, and mineral" images that keep our understanding of the Creator connected to creation. As the creed of The United Church of Canada begins, "We are not alone; we live in God's world." God has been willing to bear the image of both lion and lamb, wind and water, fire and rock, eagle and hen, vine and salt, all while being the Light of the World. With only one or two images, it's easy to have a distorted view. But with all of these images together in our box, we can hardly open our eyes without seeing the face of God.

New Images

We need to keep our boxes open to new images of God. These biblical images aren't the only ones. On any given Sunday, pastors around the country can be found giving children's sermons that present new images: "God is like this flashlight," or "God is like this teddy bear," or "God is like this bar of soap." Sometimes the images we hear don't strike us as being that benign. Some people still cannot imagine God as black or gay or even dressed in something other than a bathrobe and sandals. Maybe we need to sit with some difficult images for a while, before we rule them out. Jesus certainly encouraged his listeners to do that. Jesus must have horrified some listeners as he implied that God was like a heretical, racially mixed Samaritan.

We won't always be ready to put every image we're offered into our God-box. But if we can keep the box open—if we can keep the humility that shows us we can know God in many, many ways—we've made it easier to love and harder to judge one another.

4

Sola Scriptura

I've met a number of people who, rather than taking the Bible and putting it *in* their God-box, have allowed the Bible to *become* the God-box itself, or at least have closed their boxes with nothing else inside. This is as dangerous as it is understandable, so we need to talk at some length about it.

I have to begin by saying that I love the Bible. I've read it through, cover to cover, more times than I can remember, and I discover more every time I do it again. When I was studying Hebrew, I even became interested in the "begats"! When people ask me how they can hear God's voice, I always tell them, that at least for me, God uses Scripture more than anything else. God will often speak in the words on a page as I'm reading. At those times it seems as if those words were never there before, and they shine out as the perfect message of comfort, encouragement, answer, or—sometimes—even gentle rebuke.

Other times Bible verses come to me out of the blue, sometimes in answer to a question, but often almost as passing conversation with a God who is at my side on the journey. When I walk beside a lake that is so quiet it is almost a perfect mirror: "he leads me beside still waters" (Ps 23:2). When the birds dart around me in the trees: "Even the sparrow finds a home, and the swallow a nest for herself, where she may lay her young, at your altars, O LORD of hosts" (Ps 84:3).

In a very real way, I live in the Bible and see my world through the lens of Scripture. You may or may not agree with what I say in a sermon, but you'll always find my topic rooted in biblical sources, and leading Bible studies comes only second to preaching in my list of pastoral priorities. I love the Bible, I know it fairly well, and I've watched it transform hearts and lives. It is God's book.

What Is Truth?

Lots of Christians of all ages and stripes can assent to the phrase "the Bible is true." But what we mean by that phrase varies as widely as the people who speak it. What I mean when I say, "the Bible is true," is that I believe that the Bible accurately presents us with the truth it was meant to convey, which is the revelation of God. I don't believe that either the biblical writers or God ever meant for the Bible to be interpreted as "true" in every sense.

I believe God inspired biblical writers to convey the truth about God's nature and God's will for all of creation. When God wanted to convey truths about science, God inspired scientists. When God wanted to convey truths about history, God spoke to historians. When God wanted to convey the truth about the political and social order, God spoke to people actively studying those pursuits, and so on. That's not to say that the Bible contains nothing that is scientifically, historically, or otherwise "true." It's just that we should not be attempting to prove those sorts of truths by using the Bible, any more than we should be using science or history textbooks to prove the nature of God. The Bible wasn't even written to prove the existence of God. That God is real and active in life on Earth is already assumed from page one. The purpose of the Bible is to reveal the nature of the God who is and to show how creation is meant to respond.

As Christians, I think that becomes obvious when we think about Jesus. As the Gospel of John tells us, Jesus was "the Word made flesh." That is, when we began to muddy the message from the words of Scripture, God finally decided we needed some hands-on experience. We were hands-on learners as well as visual and auditory ones. We needed more than the Word, we needed the Word fleshed out in a human being: "God with skin on," as a common devotional has put it. So God appeared in Jesus to show us what had been said all along.

That's why we call both the Bible and Jesus the "revelation of God." As Word and flesh, they are two different forms of the same revelation. When you think about it, it's kind of ironic that we took God's gift of flesh and turned around and made it words again, continuing to ignore the testament of the body of Christ even now. The Reformation cry of "*sola scriptura*" has often made us as legalistic and rigid about the New Testament as the Pharisees had become about the Hebrew Scriptures. In many circles the Holy Spirit is held to the letter of our new law in ways that it never was in New Testament times. But that is another book. For these purposes, if we want to know what the Bible is trying to teach us, we should look at what Jesus taught, how he lived, who he blessed, and how he loved, because it is the same revelation in a whole different form. It is flesh, not word.

When we look at the life of Jesus, we discover that nobody was flocking to him to ask how old the Earth really was or which Egyptian pharaoh was in power during the Exodus. I don't recall that anyone came to him by night wanting to know if the world was created in six 24-hour periods or whether the Isaiah scroll represented the work of one, two, or three writers. Instead they came asking questions like "What must I do to inherit eternal life?" (Luke 10:25), "Who is my neighbor?" (Luke 10:29), and "Now in the law Moses commanded us to stone such women. Now what do you say?" (John 8:5). Those are exactly the types of questions we should be bringing to the Bible. Who are you, God? What should I do to be in right relationship with you and to others? Those are the questions the Bible is meant to answer, and I believe it answers them clearly and completely.

There have been times, in both contemporary and ancient cultures, when entire Christian communities have put a lid on their Bibles and made them the sum total of truth to be known. We burned scientists as heretics and made spiritual growth a fearful prospect for many others. Not long after arriving in my first church, I made a hospital visit. The man I went to see was asleep when I arrived, but a friend was sitting with him and asked me to sit down. The friend was also a member of my congregation, a man in his mid-seventies, and he was troubled.

"Let me ask you something," he began. He went on to tell me about a recent article in the paper. It had told of the discovery of some fossil or other, I don't remember now which one. "I've read a lot of things like that," said the man, "and it really seems that the scientists are right. The Earth has to be really, really old." Tears welled up in his eyes as he continued. "I guess I'm not going to be able to be a Christian anymore."

In that moment I felt the combination of grief and rage that a shepherd must feel when a wolf rips into a sheep in his flock, as I watched the pain in this precious man's eyes. And I also gained a better understanding of what Jesus was denouncing when he said to the Pharisees, "Woe to you, scribes and Pharisees, hypocrites! For you lock people out of the kingdom of heaven. For you do not go in yourselves, and when others are going in, you stop them." If Jesus was seeing what I was seeing, it's a wonder he didn't go for their throats!

Pretty strong words, but I felt then that they were appropriate. It's not to say that the scribes and Pharisees (ancient or modern) weren't sincerely trying to do what is right. But the minute they closed the lid on the God-box, the minute they looked at the Bible and moved from saying "this contains God's truth" to saying "this is the sum total of all truth," they had made an idol. And the idol gave death rather than life, both to themselves and to others.

For this troubled man, there was a happy ending. Because he was willing to ask the question, we were able to have a good discussion. He came to realize that he could have both his brain and his faith, and he reopened his box with joy. But how many others have simply done what this man had been about to do? With no room for anything but a Bible inside their God- box, then sadly, they've walked away from their faith.

All Scripture Is Inspired by God

Unfortunately, confusion about truth is only one way we turn the Bible into an idol. Let's say we agree that the Bible isn't primarily about science or history or social customs. Let's say we're united in believing that the Bible is, first and foremost, the revelation of God. There are still ways we can, to our detriment, close the lid.

Perhaps the most helpful thing I've ever learned about the Bible came from Luke Timothy Johnson, one of my seminary professors. "The Bible is not the only source of truth," he said. "It is simply the only source of truth we can agree on." That understanding opened my world. Of course the Bible couldn't contain all that could or would be revealed of God. But we needed to have some common ground to be able to have a community of faith. The Bible represents the writings that Christians of all stripes agree hold enough of the true revelation of God to be sufficient for salvation, life, and practice. That made a big difference to me.

I'd often been troubled, for example, in reading about the formation of the canon of Scripture. It was so, well, human. It's oversimplified, but the Bible was put together by committee. People got together in meetings, looked over the applicants, and decided which books were in and which ones were out. They didn't always agree. Some books that early churches had been reading and learning from didn't make it, just because the writer didn't have the right credentials. In later years, Martin Luther wanted to toss out the books of James and Revelation.

Then the Protestant churches decided that a number of the books that the Roman Catholic Church included needed to be scrapped. To this day, there are Bibles that include those books and Bibles that don't.

The absence of those latter books, which Protestants call the Apocrypha, and the Roman Catholics call the "deuterocanonical books," especially troubled me because they'd been part of Jesus' Bible and Paul's Bible. I'd read notes that even indicated that Paul made reference to some of them in his letters—letters that *were* in my Bible. At the very least they were part of what Paul meant when he said, "All scripture is inspired by God and is useful for teaching, for reproof, for correction, and for training in righteousness" (2 Tim 3:16). Suppose we'd messed up? Who's to say that God was only guiding Protestants and not Catholics? I was troubled by the whole business.

But, God bless Luke Johnson. His words fixed the problem. If the Bible as I knew it wasn't the only revelation of God, but simply the only revelation of God that we could all agree on, I could live with that quite nicely. If we disagreed on some point or other, we at least could engage the debate by agreeing that all our positions should be supported from this set of writings. This understanding freed me from concern when God spoke to me or to others through extrabiblical sources.

It should have been obvious, especially to someone who grew up in a country so enamored of free speech, that there was a fundamental problem with limiting the speech of God. But I hadn't put it in those terms before. With my new view of the Bible, I could breathe much more easily. Others who claimed to have experienced a revelation from God could well have a perspective that could help me.

God might well be speaking in the Qur'an and in the holy writings of other faiths. Since my teen years, I've been using a daily devotional edited by A. J. Russell titled *God Calling*. It claimed to be the words God spoke to two anonymous "Listeners." It almost seems miraculous that the same words touch my life in different places year after year. But I was always worried that I was giving so much credence to something that claimed to be the word of God, but that wasn't in the Bible.

With the lid off of my box, however, all that changed. The words that so often have moved me to tears and have brought me back to the God I love could still be the words of God, even though they weren't in the Bible. Since this book wasn't part of what everybody had agreed on, I needed to be sure I wasn't getting suckered into something dangerous; if it was completely opposed to the nature of God I found in the Bible, that was cause for concern. But God's speaking didn't have to be limited to words written thousands of years ago. In fact, God still might have something to say. Imagine that. I was so relieved to be able to open the box.

The World Itself Could Not Contain the Books

When I finally opened the box to allow God freedom of speech, I discovered—lo and behold!—that the concept wasn't just American. It was biblical. Just before his arrest, Jesus tells his disciples "I still have many things to say to you, but you cannot bear them now. When the Spirit of truth comes, he will guide you into all the truth" (John 16:12–13). Some people insist that the rest of what the disciples learned makes up the remainder of the New Testament. Well, where does it say that? Just because the ending of the book of Revelation says not to add to the prophecy of the book, doesn't mean that it is referring to the entire Bible. At the end of the Gospel of John, we are told, "But there are also many other things that Jesus did; if every one of them were written down, I suppose that the world itself could not contain the books that would be written" (John 21:25). John has given us only a representative sample. More was said in the past, and more will be said in the future. Don't go asking me to be the one to tell God that nothing more may be spoken. That's not a message I'm comfortable delivering to the Almighty.

I think there are two specific clues in Scripture that help us realize just how open our God-boxes are meant to be. First, there's not one but four different gospels. A lot has been written about their similarities and differences, and a fair number of people have given much of their lives to fitting them together in one narrative whole, a so-called gospel "harmony" (which harkens back to the question of whether the Bible is primarily concerned with historical detail).

But look at it this way: Jesus was a literate man. We have no reason to believe that he was not raised to read and write as any other Jewish male: in Luke 4:18–19, he reads from the Isaiah scroll in the synagogue in his hometown. If it had been important for us to know whether Jesus said in the Beatitudes, "Blessed are the poor in spirit" (Matt 5:3) or "Blessed are you who are poor" (Luke 6:20); if our salvation hung on knowing whether Jesus cleared the temple at the beginning of his ministry (John), at the end of his ministry (Matt, Mark, Luke), or twice (harmony); if his exact words and all the details were critical,

Jesus could have written them down, handed them to Peter and said, "Here, don't lose this."

But instead we've got four gospels, in which the details are different but the nature of God in Jesus is exactly the same. That encourages us to look at things in new ways, to see things from different perspectives, and maybe one day to write our own gospel of Jesus, who called us to "Come, follow me (NIV Matt 4:19)." Having four different gospels is God's way of subverting our attempts to confine Jesus to the box of Scripture. Jesus is in the box, for sure. But is he only there? I don't think so. I believe that God both has inspired the creation of Scripture and has guided its preservation. In no case do we have an original document off the chisel or pen of a biblical writer: the oldest documents we've got are copies of copies. I believe this is by God's design to help keep us from idols. Contradictions in Scripture are not proof of its falsehood, but are rather God's wry way of sticking a foot in the door of our box so that we cannot get it all the way closed.

Our second clue that Scripture is radically opposed to the notion of closed boxes is in Acts 15. Every time I read this, I wonder why we don't make more of it—why we seem to ignore the act of revolution and subversion it represents. Acts 15 describes the Council of Jerusalem, which was convened because of the conflict over the way Gentiles should convert to the faith. At its beginnings, Christianity was considered a Jewish sect, but things got trickier when the movement began attracting non-Jews.

How much of the traditional Jewish law should really be kept? While Jesus seemed to support the spirit of the law and insisted that he didn't come to abolish it, there were plenty of instances where he broke the letter of the law. Maybe, first-century Christians thought, some changes were in order. As Paul's mission to the Gentiles began to take off, conflicts began to emerge.

Did these new Gentile converts need to become Jews first in order to be called Christians? Specifically, did they need to be circumcised and follow the Jewish dietary and sacrificial laws? There was heated debate, with even Paul and Peter almost coming to blows over it, and finally church leaders got together to solve the problem once and for all: "We should not trouble those Gentiles who are turning to God, but we should write to them to abstain only from things polluted by idols and from fornication and from whatever has been strangled and from blood" (Acts 15:19–20). End of instruction.

This was momentous! The leaders of the church, almost all of them Jews, declared huge portions of the Bible no longer relevant to a new situation. They didn't require circumcision. If this decision doesn't sound so important to you, go back and read Genesis 17, which declares that circumcision is the sign of God's covenant with Abraham. Any uncircumcised male is out of the covenant and "cut off" from the people (17:14). You've got to love those biblical puns!

You'd have thought that if the council decided to retain anything, it would've been circumcision: it was the fundamental sign, after all, of God's covenant with the people. But out it went.

Why? Because the apostles and elders of the church refused to put a lid on their God-box, opening their hearts to the possibility that God was doing a new thing among them. They were swayed not by philosophical arguments or loopholes in the law, but by Peter, Paul, and Barnabas telling about their experiences.

After listening to story after story of God pouring out the Holy Spirit on uncircumcised Gentiles, the church leaders saw that if God doesn't care whether Gentiles have been circumcised or not, they shouldn't care either. They didn't condemn circumcision for those who were Jews—Paul later has Timothy circumcised to keep him in covenant with his Jewish mother—but they were open to new rules for new circumstances.

Even though they just signed a letter ignoring a good bit of Scripture, the council didn't give up the notion that their practices should be grounded in Scripture. James supported the decision with quotes from Isaiah and Amos about Gentile nations who will come to the Lord, but the general principle of their decision, James attests, is still in keeping with the law and the prophets. This, I think, is absolutely consistent with the way Jesus related to Jewish law.

What the Council of Jerusalem did resonates with at least a part of my own United Methodist heritage. The decision-making process used by John Wesley, the Anglican priest who founded Methodism, is called the "Quadrilateral." That means Wesley looked to four different things in making a decision. Scripture came first and carried the most weight: if he couldn't find scriptural support for a decision, it didn't fly.

But the Bible wasn't the only thing in Wesley's box. He considered also what was reasonable to his mind, what was observable in his experience, and what had been taught through the ages by the tradition of the church. Through the lenses of Scripture, tradition, reason, and experience, he found a balanced approach to making decisions for himself and for those in his spiritual care.

Wesley's decision to allow women to preach was, in some ways, decided by the same factors as the Council of Jerusalem. Yes, the Bible said they shouldn't, but he saw people flocking to belief in God through the preaching of women. God didn't seem to care about their gender, but only about their message. Scripture also said in Galatians 3:28 that in Christ there was no longer male and female; Wesley's mind didn't see any reason that women shouldn't preach, and although his Church tradition forbade it, God seemed wholeheartedly in favor of it. If he were to know them by their fruit, these women had fruit abundant. In the end, he decided that since at least part of Scripture could support the practice, he would rather side with what God was doing than what the organized church was doing. Wesley appointed women to preach.

At least in these things, both the early church and John Wesley were keeping an open box, believing that it was always possible for God to act in ways true to God's nature but new to our understanding. Circumcision was the way God agreed to make covenant with Israel. But who were they to say that God had to use the same covenantal signs with every nation? In short, for God to be God, there had to be freedom for God to operate in other boxes, or even outside of boxes altogether. The contents of one particular box couldn't be allowed to dictate to God, even if the contents of the box contained God's own word.

I read an article recently that quoted a clergyman defending the position of his denomination that women could not be senior pastors. He said that women who feel called to such positions are misled because "God is bound by his own word" not to issue a call that is unbiblical. I am sure this man loves God and earnestly desires both to find and to do God's will. But I would love to be a fly on the wall when he stands before God and does his best to explain that the Bible as we know and interpret it is the authority to which God must submit. "God, I know you would really like to put that woman in a church, but you know you encouraged Paul to write against it, and I'm afraid you can't take that back."

Consider instead the words of Isaiah in chapter 45:9, 11: "Woe to you who strive with your Maker, earthen vessels with the potter! Does the clay say to the one who fashions it, 'What are you making'? or 'Your work has no handles'? . . . Will you question me about my children, or command me concerning the work of my hands?" Point well taken. This will probably sound more radical than I intend, but if God is truly the author of the Bible, can't the author issue a newly revised edition? Wesley thought so, the Council of Jerusalem thought so, and probably the only thing that kept poor, old, depressed Jeremiah going was his proclamation in chapter 31:22: "For the LORD has created a new thing on the earth." (That verse continues, by the way, to say that the new thing is that "a woman encompasses a man.") If Jeremiah couldn't place his hope in God doing a completely new thing on the earth, he might well have given in to despair.

But our hope is based on the conviction that God is both willing and able to do a new thing: to take what have been only words and make them flesh, to take what has been only suffering and give it hope, to take what has become sinful through and through and, washing it, to make it brighter than snow. The very size and diversity of the Bible attest to the words of John's Gospel about the acts of God: "If every one of them were written down, I suppose that the world itself could not contain the books that would be written" (John 21:25).

My Thoughts Are Not Your Thoughts

Attempting to confine God to the sixty-six books of the Bible is not done by just one clergyman and it's not just one issue. It happens with surprising frequency. But when the lid on our God-box is also the lid of our Bible, we can do ourselves and others a great deal of damage. Not only do we turn the Bible into a weapon to tell some people that the God who can do anything cannot manage to use their particular gifts and talents. But that weapon has a kickback that also harms the wielder especially when it comes to our expectations when we pray.

I've seen people literally hold up their Bibles and shake them at God, demanding a specific action because a particular verse in the Bible seems to promise it. When this happens, I'd like to look and see what else is in their God-box. Is the entire Bible really there? What about the part where Jesus prays in the garden that this cup might pass from him and God says, "Sorry, no"? How about the part where Stephen is stoned to death, not for lack of faith but because of it. How about the part where the people of Israel were slaves in Egypt for four hundred years before God got around to sending Moses?

It's not that I don't understand. When someone you love is dying, when the rug of life has been pulled out from under you, who doesn't want to take God to task for all those promises? The book of Job always stays in my God-box because it reminds me that Job's tirade against God is a valid picture of how even the blameless respond in the face of great suffering. But every so often I need to shake up the box so that something else can come to the top. Like Isaiah 55:8, for instance: "For my thoughts are not your thoughts, nor are your ways my ways, says the LORD."

When we attempt to bind God by the words of the Bible, we cause ourselves needless pain. I could save hours and hours of counseling time if I didn't have to talk people through the faith crises that come about when God refuses to perform on demand. It's not necessarily the person's own arrogance that has caused the problem: sometimes it's merely what they've been taught.

One woman actually had been told that the reason her daughter died was that she hadn't been able to muster enough faith to have her prayers for healing answered! That's what the Bible says, she was told: have faith and do not doubt and you can make mountains move. So if your mountain doesn't move, it's your own fault. Somehow, I don't think that's what God had in mind.

God Is Love

Am I saying that God's promises are just nice words that can't be taken seriously? Not at all. But we need to remember that in God we live and move and have our being—not the other way round. I believe that every prayer of faith is answered. Sometimes the answer is "Yes," sometimes it's "No," and sometimes it's "Maybe" or "Wait awhile." Our purposes and desires are considered and even sometimes granted just because we happen to want them: that's the absolute wonder of being in relationship with a God who is willing to get personally involved with us and love us. But when we fail to accept an answer we don't like and recognize that it just might be possible that God has purposes that we can't know or understand, we've crossed the line.

The most comforting claim in the Bible, to me, is not "Ask, and it will be given you," (Matt 7:7) or any of the verses like it. It is, "God is love" (1 John 4:8). My father died suddenly of a heart attack at age forty-seven. It was midnight and we were all home and asleep. I woke to the commotion of my mother almost screaming to the emergency personnel on the phone, "He won't wake up! He won't wake up!"

When I ran down to their bedroom, I knelt down by my motionless father and prayed for his life.

At the time, I was very much a literalist in my approach to Scripture. It said that Jesus raised the dead, and that Jesus' disciples would be able to do everything that he did and even greater things. And so I prayed for resurrection. Hard. With faith. In Jesus' name. And, just as I felt myself moving over the edge from intense prayer to hysteria, I got an answer that was as uncomplicated as my faith. I literally felt a hand on my shoulder and heard a voice say, "No."

Then the miracle happened. It wasn't the miracle of resurrection that I had asked for. It wasn't the miracle of hearing God's voice or feeling God's hand. It was the miracle of being flooded with the peace that passes all understanding. It was years later that I told my mother what had gone on in that room as she finished her phone call and rushed downstairs to look for the ambulance. But when I finally did tell her the story, she explained that the peace was not just mine: in that same moment, it had reached down to her as well on the floor below.

Our faith isn't that we get what we want, or even that we learn to want what we get. I grieve for my father, still. But our faith is that "neither death, nor life, nor angels, nor rulers, nor things present, nor things to come, nor powers, nor height, nor depth, nor anything else in all creation, will be able to separate us from the love of God in Christ Jesus our Lord." All of God's promises are possible at any time, and it isn't wrong to pray for the desires of our hearts. But the Bible is a tool to help us know and love God better, not a law book by which God must abide. God hears our prayers and answers with love.

The Open Bible

I've always said that when I finally meet God face to face, I'll find some of my sermons in God's filing cabinet and others on the dartboard. God's word on what I've preached and taught in my lifetime probably will begin with, "I know you meant well, but . . ." That said, however, I still think that confusing a revelation of God that has been reduced to words with the fullness of the God that it reveals is both foolhardy and dangerous. God doesn't have to do what I say, even if I can back it up with Scripture. Otherwise there's a reversal of authority with which I'm not at all comfortable.

I suppose if we were to look at all the ways the Bible could become an idol, the world couldn't contain the books that would be written.

This much will have to do: put the Bible in your box, by all means. But remember that the Bible isn't God but rather the revelation of God put into human terms—and that means, by definition, limited terms. It reveals the source of all truth rather than disclosing all truths. It discloses the law of God not the law for God. The Bible was made for people, not people for the Bible. That's why the Bible on our altars always lies wide open.

5

Who Then Can Be Saved?

One of my favorite discussion starters in Sunday school classes is, "What if you get to heaven and discover that, due to a deathbed conversion, the guy with the mansion next to yours is Adolf Hitler?" I find in those classes that most people have difficulty with at least some aspect of God's grace and forgiveness. There are some folks we hope God isn't ever going to forgive, no matter how sorry they might have become. We close the lid on God's freedom to forgive, deciding for ourselves who should receive mercy and who should receive justice.

But as understandably troubled as many people are at the thought of Hitler making heaven, the discomfort sometimes runs much deeper when I suggest that maybe God would let in people from other faiths or—perish the thought!—someone of no professed faith at all. I will leave it to psychologists to explain why we seem to have this deep need to know and to name who is "in" and who is "out" of God's heaven. But whatever the reason, that's what we do. We often have a lid on our boxes with a salvation-shaped hole, and no ill-fitting pegs need apply.

I had a lid like that once. I was only doing what I believed the Bible taught, and I thought that seeing the world in terms of those who were "in" and those who were "out" was simply the way it was. My teenage evangelism efforts reflected that, and at night I was often inconsolable as I wrestled and cried with God over people I loved who weren't—it seemed to me—"saved."

My own best friend, Celeste, had left the Roman Catholic Church and was a professed "free thinker." My intense efforts to save her from the fires of hell only ended up making hell start a bit earlier for her, as I was insufferable in my attempts to reshape her in a way that would make her fit through my lid. It is a tribute to her love and forbearance that we are still friends after thirty years, and in many ways this book is my act of repentance for the pain and suffering I caused her during that time in our lives.

I know in most cases such things are done sincerely and often with much pain and anguish. That's the way it was with me. But I believe now that much of that pain and anguish is unnecessary. I want to set free people who think like I once thought: free to revel in God's vast embrace rather than cowering before the fear that those we love are destined for fire and damnation.

In Romans 9–11, Paul deals with the same issues as he wrestles with the fact that God first chose Israel and then later called Gentiles into the fold, too. Is God fickle? That's the question at the root of the book of Romans. If Israel is "in," doesn't that mean Gentiles are "out"? Has God suddenly switched sides and now Israel is out of favor? Most of all, if God seems so capricious, can we trust God's promises? Of course, says Paul. The purpose of Jesus, he seems to say, is to allow for the Gentiles to be chosen in addition to—not in place of—Israel. Jesus, in other words, takes the lid off of Israel's box. There are far more people who can rightly be numbered among "God's people" than anybody ever guessed. And for anyone who finds this disturbing, Paul quotes God's words to Moses back in Exodus 33:19 and reminds the Romans in 9:15–16 that God said, "'I will have mercy on whom I have mercy, and I will have compassion on whom I have compassion.' So it depends not on human will or exertion, but on God who shows mercy."

Who gets saved is, thankfully, up to God and not us. If only I'd heard that verse when I was a teenager. If only I'd heard God gently—or not so gently—reminding me that there was no formula for salvation that could bind God, and that all my fears were based on a limited interpretation of just a few verses of Scripture. I think I'd have been better off—and I know some of my friends would've been much better off—if God had risen up in wrath and thundered, "Who do you think you are that you can be so sure who will and won't receive my mercy? I will have mercy on whomever I want and compassion wherever I please and no human being reciting Bible verses at me can change it!" If only I could've seen that in naming some as being outside the bounds of God's mercy, I was trying to usurp the authority and freedom of God.

We can, I believe, have assurances about our own salvation as our relationship with God grows and deepens. But for me to presume to make definite judgments about how others will fare in that regard now seems presumptuous at best. These days I don't share my faith to keep others from hell. I share my faith now because it transformed my life and held me up when all else has let me down. I want others to have that, too. I tell people they need to meet God for the same reasons that I tell people they need to meet my brother, Rob: because I think he's the coolest thing since sliced bread. The wonder is that I enjoy being an evangelist now, and I find that my friends no longer cover their heads or their ears when the subject of religion comes up. Paul's instruction to Timothy is important to remember. In 1 Timothy 2:4, Paul tells Timothy to pray and intercede and give thanks for all those in high positions because God "desires everyone to be saved and to come to the knowledge of the truth." Before we actually delve into interpretations of specific Bible verses, I have to wonder whether our own hearts are in order: if we, like God, actually want others to be saved. It's easy sometimes to want salvation for vague groups of others, but what about specific, real-life others: the nasty coworker, the abusive family member, the kid I don't want my kids seen with, the politician who stands for everything I find despicable, the groups that believe and think differently than I do. Put aside for the moment the question of whether everyone will *actually* be saved. Do we truly *want* everyone to be saved?

If you have trouble with this, read the book of Jonah. It's a classic rendering of the reluctant evangelist. Jonah refuses God's call to go to Nineveh simply because Jonah hates the Ninevites. He doesn't want to tell them to repent because he's afraid they will and that God will save them. He'd much rather see them obliterated, consumed by fire and sulphur like the residents of Sodom and Gomorrah. Even when God strong-arms Jonah and he finally reaches the city, he hates the Ninevites as much as ever—even when they repent and turn to God. Jonah, furious, plunks himself down on the outskirts of town to pout until he dies. He simply can't stand that God is merciful to the people of Nineveh. God should have higher standards.

It is my prayer that even those who still believe that it's appropriate to close the box and limit God's prerogative to save will close that box with sorrow. If there are people from Nineveh in your life, whether they're individuals or categories of people, pray that you might receive the heart of God that at least wants to save them all. That is the place to begin. Otherwise, God might send you, like Jonah, off to spend some time with fish innards—an experience I don't recommend.

But the Bible Says . . .

I don't argue that salvation is universally granted. I don't believe that universally available and universally applied necessarily go together. I believe the former but find no biblical support for the latter, and I'm enough of a Wesleyan that I need at least some scriptural grounding for an idea. But here's the point: the only person whose salvation I'm in a position to be assured of is me. Lots of people, though, are stymied by some of the biblical passages about God's saving some and not others. So let's take a closer look at exactly what the Bible does say about who's in and who's out of the kingdom, and why I think that, taken together, those passages show that we should leave the box closing up to God.

When we start looking to the Bible to answer the question, "What must I do to be saved?" we quickly discover that the answers vary, sometimes by quite a bit. Some passages talk about an inner attitude of the heart while others talk of deeds of justice and mercy: the age-old tension between faith and works.

While different Christians duke it out over salvation by faith or salvation by works, each with solid passages to back them up, I have to step back from the fray and say, "Hey, wait a minute! If we believe that God guided and preserved this set of writings, then there was a reason that God kept all these conflicting passages hanging together. Maybe it's not one or the other, but both of them together." Maybe James was right when he wrote, "Faith without works is dead."

So let's consider some important passages in each of these categories, works and faith. We'll look at what each says about salvation, and then we will see if there is some way to tie them together or if we simply have to hold them in tension and let God do the final sorting. We'll go first to some of the more well-known passages that indicate salvation by works.

The Rich Young Man

Matthew 19:16–30

> Then someone came to him and said, "Teacher, what good deed must I do to have eternal life?" And he said to him, "Why do you ask me about what is good? There is only one who is good. If you wish to enter into life, keep the commandments."

He said to him, "Which ones?" And Jesus said, "You shall not murder; You shall not commit adultery; You shall not steal; You shall not bear false witness; Honor your father and mother; also, You shall love your neighbor as yourself." The young man said to him, "I have kept all these, what do I still lack?" Jesus said to him, "If you wish to be perfect, go, sell your possessions, and give the money to the poor, and you will have treasure in heaven; then come, follow me." When the young man heard this word, he went away grieving, for he had many possessions.

Then Jesus said to his disciples, "Truly I tell you, it will be hard for a rich person to enter the kingdom of heaven. Again I tell you, it is easier for a camel to go through the eye of a needle than for someone who is rich to enter the kingdom of God." When the disciples heard this, they were greatly astounded and said, "Then who can be saved?" But Jesus looked at them and said, "For mortals it is impossible, but for God all things are possible."

Then Peter said in reply, "Look, we have left everything and followed you. What then will we have?" Jesus said to them, "Truly I tell you, at the renewal of all things, when the Son of Man is seated on the throne of his glory, you who have followed me will also sit on twelve thrones, judging the twelve tribes of Israel. And everyone who has left houses or brothers or sisters or father or mother or children or fields, for my name's sake, will receive a hundredfold, and will inherit eternal life. But many who are first will be last, and the last will be first.

"Then who can be saved?" the disciples ask in Matthew 19:25. Their question comes in response to Jesus' statement that it's easier for a camel to go through the eye of a needle than for the rich to enter the kingdom. And that pronouncement comes, in turn, in response to the rich young man in verse 16 who asks, "Teacher, what good deed must I do to have eternal life?" Those are both different forms of the same question about what it takes to be saved, so let's look at Jesus' answer to each.

To the rich young man Jesus says, "If you wish to enter into life, keep the commandments." But which ones exactly? Jesus refers to the Ten Commandments by quoting several of them, and throwing in the commandment from Leviticus 19:18 about loving your neighbor as yourself. Check. Check. Been there, the young man insists. Done that. "What now?" the young man wants to know. So then Jesus kicks it up a notch. He moves the question from eternal life to perfection—in Wesleyan language, from justifying to sanctifying grace—and tells the young man that to be perfect he must go and sell all he has and give the money to the poor. Then, rather than just building up his wealth all over again, he could make a true lifestyle change and follow Jesus as a disciple. That will give him not only a place in heaven but treasure in heaven as well. But the man can't do this last thing. Easier, Jesus says, for a camel to pass through the eye of a needle.

Think about this: not a word does Jesus say to this young man about the things he needs to believe. Jesus doesn't not respond to his "What must I *do*" question with "Fool, salvation is by faith, not works." Jesus gives him the requirements for what he must do, and as it turns out, everything he needed to know about salvation he'd already learned in Hebrew school. Obey the commandments and love your neighbor as yourself. It's that simple. Discipleship— following and learning from Jesus—has a role in perfection (or sanctification, if you will) but the point is that the "Come, follow me" line of this story is only spoken because the young man pressed the issue about perfection. "If you wish to enter into life, keep the commandments" was the answer to the young man's question. Works. Even if you include the selling of all his possessions as part of what is necessary for salvation, it is still works. There's not a doctrine question in here.

Then the disciples ask Jesus the same two-part question. Dismayed by Jesus saying that the rich cannot enter the Kingdom of God— maybe they haven't completely emptied their bank accounts?—they ask in desperation, "Then who can be saved?" Here's another opportunity for Jesus to plug himself. He doesn't. Instead he puts salvation decisions squarely in the hands of God by saying, "For mortals it is impossible, but for God all things are possible." That's an open-box statement if I ever heard one. It's also where salvation by works and salvation by grace meet. It's works that do it, and God's grace that makes the works possible.

The last few verses of chapter 19 illustrate the benefits that come from following Jesus. When the disciples remind Jesus of just how much they've given up to follow him, Jesus responds that anyone who has left "houses or brothers or sisters or father or mother or children or fields, for my name's sake, will receive a hundredfold, and will inherit eternal life. But many who are first will be last, and the last will be first."

It's true that becoming a faithful disciple of Jesus will get you eternal life: Jesus says that. But what Jesus *doesn't* seem to say is that the reverse is also true: that those who don't take the further step of leaving all to become disciples of Jesus won't inherit eternal life. Salvation in this passage rests squarely on a person's deeds, enabled by God, and in that regard the rich young man has made it. In verse 30 the statement about the first and the last makes it sound, to me at least, that both the rich young man and the disciples will share in the kingdom, but that the disciples have an advantage that will bring them in before those (like the young man) who don't go the second mile of giving up life's comforts to follow Jesus.

For my more liberal readers, that interpretation can still smack of domination and privilege paradigms. Talk of "first" and "last" doesn't sit well with those who work for an egalitarian society. But if first and last are about timing rather than hierarchy, I think the teeth are removed. If we remember that Jesus said the Kingdom of God is within us, and if we consider that eternal life begins here on earth rather than after death, the business about first and last need only reference how long it takes for the light of God's love to dawn in our hearts. Those who drop everything and put all of their resources toward finding God will, simply speaking, find God first: just like full-time students get a degree before part-time students, even though they begin together. First and last don't indicate a preference on God's part for one or another, but simply refer to the timetable of those who need to hang onto the world a bit longer.

The Good Samaritan
Luke 10:25–37

Just then a lawyer stood up to test Jesus. "Teacher," he said, "what must I do to inherit eternal life?" He said to him, "What is written in the law? What do you read there?" He answered, "You shall love the Lord your God with all your heart, and with all your soul, and with all your strength, and with all your mind; and your neighbor as yourself." And he said to him, "You have given the right answer; do this, and you will live."

But wanting to justify himself, he asked Jesus, "And who is my neighbor?" Jesus replied, "A man was going down from Jerusalem to Jericho, and fell into the hands of robbers, who stripped him, beat him, and went away, leaving him half dead. Now by chance a priest was going down that road; and when he saw him, he passed by on the other side. So likewise a Levite, when he came to the place and saw him, passed by on the other side. But a Samaritan while traveling came near him; and when he saw him, he was moved with pity. He went to him and bandaged his wounds, having poured oil and wine on them. Then he put him on his own animal, brought him to an inn, and took care of him. The next day he took out two denarii, gave them to the innkeeper, and said, 'Take care of him; and when I come back, I will repay you whatever more you spend.' Which of these three, do you think, was a neighbor to the man who fell into the hands of the robbers?" He said, "The one who showed him mercy." Jesus said to him, "Go and do likewise."

The litmus test of who can be saved is not something unique to the Christian faith. The Jews of Jesus' day had their notions as well, and in Luke 10:25, a lawyer stands up with a question to "test" Jesus. The test question? "What must I do to inherit eternal life?"

In response, Jesus turns the question back on the asker. "What is written in the law?" he asks. "What do you read there?" The man responds with the combined words from Deuteronomy 6:5 and Leviticus 19:18 that Christians have come to call the Great Commandment: "You shall love the Lord your God with all your heart, and with all your soul, and with all your strength, and with all your mind; and your neighbor as yourself." How does Jesus respond? He commends him. "You have given the right answer; do this, and you will live." Works through and through.

It's the same answer Jesus gave the rich young man. Everything anybody needed for salvation is in the five books of Moses. Love God (Deut 6:5)—the focus of the first tablet of the Ten Commandments. Love your neighbor as yourself (Lev 19:18)—the focus of the second tablet. Like the rich young man, this lawyer also wanted to push the envelope, so he asked who his neighbor was. His answer was the parable of the Good Samaritan.

The parable of the Good Samaritan probably had the same effect on the Jews of Jesus' day that thinking about non-Christians in heaven does to many Christians today. The Samaritans were the heretics who had the doctrine all wrong, who had intermarried and sullied the race, who worshiped in the wrong temple.

Samaritans and Jews would go to extraordinary lengths to avoid one another. So imagine how this lawyer might have felt when Jesus turned a Samaritan into the hero of his story. Only the Samaritan understands the simple command to "love your neighbor as yourself" when both a priest and a Levite do not. In this parable, Jesus pries the box open with the biggest crowbar around, and the lawyer probably wished he had been content with his first answer and kept his mouth shut.

The Judgment of the Nations
Matthew 25:31–46

"When the Son of Man comes in his glory, and all the angels with him, then he will sit on the throne of his glory. All the nations will be gathered before him, and he will separate people one from another as a shepherd separates the sheep from the goats, and he will put the sheep at his right hand and the goats at the left. Then the king will say to those at his right hand, 'Come you that are blessed by my Father, inherit the kingdom prepared for you from the foundation of the world; for I was hungry and you gave me food, I was thirsty and you gave me something to drink, I was a stranger and you welcomed me, I was naked and you gave me clothing, I was sick and you took care of me, I was in prison and you visited me.' Then the righteous will answer him, 'Lord, when was it that we saw you hungry and gave you food, or thirsty and gave you something to drink? And when was it that we saw you a stranger and welcomed you, or naked and gave you clothing? And when was it that we saw you sick or in prison and visited you?' And the king will answer them, 'Truly I tell you, just as you did it to one of the least of these who are members of my family, you did it to me.' Then he will say to those at his left hand, 'You that are accursed, depart from me into the eternal fire prepared for the devil and his angels; for I was hungry and you gave me no food, I was thirsty and you gave me nothing to drink, I was a stranger and you did not welcome me, naked and you did not give me clothing, sick and in prison and you did not visit me.' Then they also will answer, 'Lord, when was it that we saw you hungry or thirsty or a stranger or naked or sick or in prison, and did not take care of you?' Then he will answer them, 'Truly I tell you, just as you did not do it to one of the least of these, you did not do it to me.' And these will go away into eternal punishment, but the righteous into eternal life."

Although this passage in Matthew doesn't come in answer to a specific question about salvation, it does come at the end of a section crammed full of examples of what people could expect at a final judgment. Final things are on Jesus' mind just two days before his last Passover. The tone has been getting darker since the cleansing of the temple back in chapter 21 and the gentle beatitudes of the early chapters have given way to harsh curses—on unfruitful fig trees, on hypocritical Pharisees and Scribes. Jesus laments over the state of Jerusalem and then begins to predict the destruction of the temple and the end of the age. It's after these predictions and the commands to be watchful that we get scenes of judgment.

At the end of chapter 24 the slave who does his master's work is the one who will be rewarded, while the slave who "begins to beat his fellow slaves, and eats and drinks with drunkards" gets put into the "weeping and gnashing of teeth" category. Works. Chapter 25, opening with another warning to be prepared, follows with two more descriptions of what earns either God's favor or God's wrath. The first is the parable of the talents, beginning in 25:14, where the ones who are rewarded are those whose good stewardship has multiplied God's gifts. And the ones who never use what they've been given for the benefit of God's kingdom? They'll be gnashing their teeth with the wicked slave from the previous chapter. Works again.

And then comes verse 31, which sounds not so much like a parable but rather a simple description of what God wants from us. Sit down and read it through; it couldn't be plainer. The blessed are the ones who fed the hungry, watered the thirsty, welcomed the stranger, clothed the naked, cared for the sick, and visited the imprisoned. The cursed are the ones who ignored all those needs. It's the "love your neighbor" command spelled out in more detail. It's what the Good Samaritan did.

In this, as in all of the above, it seems that Jesus validates the words of the prophet Micah who said in 6:8, "He has told you, O mortal, what is good; and what does the LORD require of you but to do justice, and to love kindness, and to walk humbly with your God?" Whatever answer we find when we wrestle with the question "Then who can be saved?"

we do violence to huge portions of Scripture if our answer does not include works of any kind.

But that's only part of the story.

I Am the Way
John 14:1–11

> "Do not let your hearts be troubled. Believe in God, believe also in me. In my Father's house there are many dwelling places. If it were not so, would I have told you that I go to prepare a place for you? And if I go and prepare a place for you, I will come again and will take you to myself, so that where I am, there you may be also. And you know the way to the place where I am going." Thomas said to him, "Lord, we do not know where you are going. How can we know the way?" Jesus said to him, "I am the way, and the truth, and the life. No one comes to the Father except through me. If you know me, you will know my Father also. From now on you do know him and have seen him."
>
> Philip said to him, "Lord, show us the Father, and we will be satisfied." Jesus said to him, "Have I been with you all this time, Philip, and you still do not know me? Whoever has seen me has seen the Father. How can you say, 'Show us the Father'? Do you not believe that I am in the Father and the Father is in me? The words that I say to you I do not speak on my own; but the Father who dwells in me does his works. Believe me that I am in the Father and the Father is in me; but if you do not, then believe me because of the works themselves."

This passage fascinates me. It could be used so many different ways, but mostly it's just read at funerals. Seldom do I hear talk of the "many mansions" or "rooms" or "dwelling places" or whatever your translation uses. "In my Father's house are many rooms" (NIV) reminds me of the passages that talk of sheep in other folds and Jesus making room for the children. It seems like one more place where God indicates that the box is open and there is room for those we don't see in our particular "room," the physical or spiritual location where we are. Most of the time, the focus of this passage is shifted down a few verses to "no one comes to the Father except through me," which tends to make me imagine that all those lovely rooms are sitting empty while people wander lost, trying to find the only door.

I'm not sure when I realized it, but at some point I came to under-stand that my reading of this section had been limited by the uniformity of interpretation in the circles where I traveled. So I took the verse out of its traditional home and looked at what it actually said for a moment. I found in doing that—reading it as if I were reading it for the first time—I learned something completely different. Suppose that by saying "I am the way" Jesus means something like "by my agency." In other words, suppose Jesus is the means by which we reach the Father in the same way that our lungs, for example, are the means by which we breathe. When I was born, some rude doctor slapped me, and I took my first breath. I didn't know the first bit about lungs. I didn't know or understand the means by which that breath was possible, but in the perfect design of God, I didn't need to. I simply obeyed a natural impulse and breath was mine. Nevertheless, I couldn't have done it without lungs. Lungs were the only way I could breathe.

Well, suppose Jesus is connected to salvation that same way. Suppose that the work of Jesus in his birth, death, and resurrection is the thing that makes it possible for all human beings to be in intimate relationship with God once again. That could mean that anyone who ended up in loving relationship with God had done so by means of Jesus. They may or may not know their benefactor. They may not even believe it when they're told, just as young children sometimes have a hard time believing the biology of how they came to be here. But the facts are the same, whether they're believed or not. Jesus could be the "way" simply because he was the agent that made it possible.

Or how about this? Jesus could be the only way to God because as human beings we can only really know and love God by experiencing God in human form. "Jesus is the only way" could mean that God incarnate in human flesh is the only way. That might mean our connection to Jesus of Nazareth through the Bible's record of him. But it might also refer to our connection to Jesus through the "least of these" as described in Matthew 25. It might reflect the reality written in 1 John 4:20–21 that insists that we have no business talking about loving God if we can't manage to love our brothers and sisters in the flesh, and it could give real responsibility to the church as the Body of Christ. "No one comes to the Father except through me" could refer to the human reality that as bodily creatures we need to come to God through Incarnation. We need God "with skin on" for the reality of

God's love to be manifest, and the lack of faith we condemn in others might bounce right back and condemn the lack of Christ in us instead.

Both of those possible interpretations affirm the truth of the verse that Jesus is the only way, while also keeping the box open for those who have not openly professed Jesus. Again, I do not intend to say that there are no criteria for judgment (all of these passages are conditional in one way or another), merely that those criteria are more difficult to identify than we may have thought.

For God So Loved the World
John 3:16–21

> "For God so loved the world that he gave his only Son, so that everyone who believes in him may not perish but may have eternal life.
>
> Indeed, God did not send the Son into the world to condemn the world, but in order that the world might be saved through him. Those who believe in him are not condemned; but those who do not believe are condemned already, because they have not believed in the name of the only Son of God. And this is the judgment, that the light has come into the world, and people loved darkness rather than light because their deeds were evil. For all who do evil hate the light and do not come to the light, so that their deeds may not be exposed. But those who do what is true come to the light, so that it may be clearly seen that their deeds have been done in God."

The verse that begins this passage is the mother of all salvation verses, and taken by itself it doesn't close the box. It affirms that those who believe in Jesus shall inherit eternal life. At least for the purposes of this book, that has never been at issue. The question has been whether the Bible truly insists that those who don't believe won't inherit eternal life, and further down in this passage we hit trouble. Verse 18 says, "Those who believe in him are not condemned; but those who do not believe are condemned already, because they have not believed in the name of the only Son of God." Ouch. And yet the verse right before that asserts that "God did not send the Son into the world to condemn the world, but in order that the world might be saved through him."

It's fair to say that Jesus doesn't address the entirety of the human condition in every sentence. He didn't teach in a vacuum but in a very particular time and place. Sometimes the situation called for him to say something like "Whoever is not against you is for you" in Luke 9:50, when just a couple of chapters later the situation called for him to turn that on its head and say, "Whoever is not with me is against me" (Luke 11:23). Purists panic and think that Jesus is contradicting himself, but it can simply mean that Jesus is not always speaking words that are appropriate for all times, places, and circumstances. Sometimes he does, but not always. In Jesus we are witnessing a human life, not a theology textbook. Most often, I think, Jesus adjusts his words and his emphases to match the particular person or situation in front of him at the time.

When I read these verses from John with that in mind, the waters clear a bit. Jesus is talking to a very particular person here. He is speaking to Nicodemus, a Pharisee who has come to Jesus by night to express his faith that Jesus comes from God. Jesus praises his insight by telling him that he wouldn't have been able to discern this if he hadn't been born again, or born from above.

The language confuses Nicodemus, who can't get beyond thinking about a literal birth, so Jesus explains to him the difference between physical birth (of water) and spiritual birth. In that same context, Jesus goes on to describe to this Jewish teacher and leader other things about Jesus' own nature, purpose, and work. Nicodemus has established the context of the conversation by talking about his own decision to accept that Jesus' work is divine in nature.

It's not a problem for me to look at the later verses when I keep that context in mind. For those who have met Jesus face to face, for those who have been watching his work, for those with all the benefit of the revelation of God in the law and the prophets—for them to fail to believe that Jesus comes in the name of God is blasphemy. As Nicodemus proclaims back in verse 2, "No one can do these signs that you do apart from the presence of God." That is obvious to anyone who has truly studied the Scriptures. Those who had a real relationship with the God of Israel automatically recognized the same personality in Jesus. To look at the signs of God's love that are evident in Jesus' miracles and proclaim them not of God is to deny the nature of God.

When Jesus says, "Those who do not believe are condemned already, because they have not believed in the name of the only Son of God," he's talking about "those" in the circles in which Nicodemus travels: the Scribes and the Pharisees who claim to have the corner on how to spot God's activity and to know God's will. Those who are able to recognize the works and words of Jesus as coming from God give evidence of spiritual birth in their lives that enables them to see the Kingdom of God. But those who can't recognize the healing of a blind man as the work of God show their own blindness and unloving nature. To look at an act of love and name it as an act of the devil shows a person to be in darkness already.

It's no surprise that Jesus, in both Matthew and Mark, says that declaring that the works of God are the works of the devil is an unpardonable sin: I suppose because even God can't pardon someone who won't repent. If it's love in some way, shape, or form that moves us to repentance—and if we boot love out of our lives and call it evil—what's left? That discussion is out of the scope of this book, but I think that general framework could form the context for understanding John 3 in a less exclusive way. This is not a discussion about pagans in second-century Norway, but a discussion about Jewish teachers in first-century Palestine—Jesus' own place and time. Jesus' words here speak about the way that these teachers have—or haven't—responded to his ministry. I believe all those who recognize Jesus as rabbi, prophet, or generally someone who did the work of God on earth have passed the test of John 3.

Justified by Faith

Romans 3:21–26

> But now, apart from law, the righteousness of God has been disclosed, and is attested by the law and the prophets, the righteousness of God through faith in Jesus Christ for all who believe. For there is no distinction, since all have sinned and fall short of the glory of God; they are now justified by his grace as a gift, through the redemption that is in Christ Jesus, whom God put forward as a sacrifice of atonement by his blood, effective through faith. He did this to show his righteousness, because in his divine forbearance he had passed over the sins previously committed; it was to prove at the present time that he himself is righteous and that he justifies the one who has faith in Jesus.

As any student of church history can tell you, this is the passage that blew the lid off of Martin Luther's box. Having struggled all of his life to be saved by his good works, this passage finally opened Luther's eyes to see that he wasn't completely responsible for his own salvation. The righteousness of God was available "as a gift, through the redemption that is in Christ Jesus, whom God put forward as a sacrifice of atonement by his blood, effective through faith" (Rom 3:24–25). From this new awareness came one of the rallying cries of the Reformation and of Protestantism ever since: "*Sola Fides!*" or "Faith alone!"

While I can appreciate what this passage did for Luther, especially given his personal history, I think he jumped too far in the opposite direction when he threw all of the works passages out of his box and closed the lid on faith alone. He truly wanted to wipe out every reference to works as it related to salvation, even calling the book of James a "straw epistle" because of its emphasis on works. But this way of thinking swaps the abuses of one extreme for the abuses of the other, and perhaps Luther would have been kinder to both Jews and peasants had he kept his box at least partly open to the notion of salvation by works. And yet the power of this passage inspired John Wesley to realize that God was more gracious than he'd imagined. We've truly missed the mark if we don't recognize the truth of these words: we cannot save ourselves. God has reached out to us through Jesus in the greatest act of love that the world has known, and this act makes it possible for us to stand in the presence of God.

So why do I think Luther went too far in tossing good works out of the box? Because of what Paul says in verse 31: "Do we then overthrow the law by this faith? By no means! On the contrary, we uphold the law." Paul didn't toss the law out of his box because of this concept, and we shouldn't either. Somehow they go together.

To begin with, the phrase in verses 22 and 26 that is often translated "faith *in* Jesus" can just as well be translated "faith *of* Jesus." It's a little word that makes a big difference. Whose faith is it that saves us? The focus, at least of this passage, is what God did for us in Jesus rather than what we do ourselves by faith. We have to be careful that faith doesn't become simply another work that we need to do to be saved. It was the faithful obedience of Jesus to the will of God that resulted in the opportunity for our salvation. This act of atonement in Jesus is how we are justified in seeking access to the presence of God.

Yet the passage does talk of believing as a response we must make and, even with translating the phrase "faith of Jesus" in verse 26, it's still a faith that we ourselves must possess. So what do we do with this? I think it helps to look at the nature of faith and belief. I'm not sure how it happened, but we seem to have disconnected what we believe from how we behave. Somewhere along the line, we began to talk about belief as a purely intellectual process so that people got the impression that one could "believe" in God without necessarily having that belief impact life in any significant way. We could have faith that Jesus was really God's Son in the same way we had faith that rocks were really a collection of atoms and other things too small to see. It was nice to be "in the know" but it made no real difference in the way most people related to rocks.

The Bible, I believe, is more holistic. When the Bible talks about faith in Jesus or belief in the faith of Jesus, it's talking about something intimately connected to our behavior. We see that in Hebrews 11:1 (KJV): "Faith is the substance of things hoped for, the evidence of things not seen." Faith is substance and evidence. The faith part is something that can be seen and experienced, even if the object of faith cannot be known this way.

If I actually believe that my house is going to burn down in the morning, you'll see the evidence of my belief in the way I drag out the furniture and spray the house with water. If I sit quietly in a café telling you my house will burn down, you can see the evidence of the insurance I hope for—and it might be wise to have me investigated for arson. But in any case, faith is the evidence we show that the thing in which we have placed our faith is true.

Our religious faith is "evidenced" in a number of ways. We share the bread and the cup together in Communion to give substance to our hope of one day feasting together at God's heavenly banquet. We evidence the unseen cleansing of God with the visible waters of baptism. We proclaim our faith that God dwells in human flesh as we feed the hungry, clothe the naked, and see in the prison inmate the eyes of Jesus. Faith, even as we know it, is not unconnected to works.

I would go further and say that faith and works are actually the same thing. It sounds odd to say it that way because we have so divorced thinking and doing. But suppose we express "faith" as "fidelity," which is one of its meanings in Greek, or in the more Hebrew-oriented "faithfulness." Both of those words express not a construct of the mind but an attitude of the heart evidenced in deeds. Is the fish symbol on the bumper of your car completely unrelated to the way you drive? Do you think it's unrelated in the mind of the person you just cut off? "I will show you my faith by what I do," says James (NIV 2:18).

Everyone Who Loves Is Born of God

1 John 4:7–12

> Beloved, let us love one another, because love is from God; everyone who loves is born of God and knows God. Whoever does not love does not know God, for God is love. God's love was revealed among us in this way: God sent his only Son into the world so that we might live through him. In this is love, not that we loved God but that he loved us and sent his Son to be the atoning sacrifice for our sins. Beloved, since God loved us so much, we also ought to love one another. No one has ever seen God; if we love one another, God lives in us, and his love is perfected in us.

This segment of 1 John puts it all together nicely. We might wrestle with nuances in meaning among faith and fidelity and faithfulness, but this passage puts it much more simply: "Everyone who loves is born of God and knows God. Whoever does not love does not know God, for God is love." Love is a word that expresses it all at once: the inner attitude of the heart, which can't help but overflow into the actions of everyday life. Anyone who has ever been in a relationship can tell you that if the words "I love you" aren't at some point backed up by loving action, the truth of the proclamation is called into question. Real love acts: not out of duty, but because it has no other choice. It is part of what it means to love.

Love sums up all of the salvation by works passages, which is why Jesus made the triune love of God, neighbor, and self the commandment that is greater than all the others. In verses 9 and following of 1 John 4, the passage goes on to show how love is also related to the faith passages. Jesus was the revelation of God's love for us (v. 9). It's not our love for God that saves us, but God's love for us (v. 10). When we truly believe that, we can't help but respond in kind by loving one another (v. 11). In fact, it's in doing this that we make God visible to one

another and engage in a practice—loving God and our neighbor—
that will make us perfect (v. 12).

Faith without Works Is Dead

So it seems to me that the statement of James in 2:17 that "Faith by
itself, if it has no works is dead" is really the same as Paul saying in 1
Corinthians 13:2 (NASB), "If I have all faith so as to remove mountains, but do not have love, I am nothing." Our works are as necessary
as the earlier passages indicated, but to save us they must be motivated
by love. Although God has knowledge by which to judge, we do not.
Our boxes have to stay open. We can see the works, but that's only part
of the picture. We cannot know the depths of another person's heart.

We can see enough to judge whether we want to associate with a
person. We can see enough to set boundaries for behavior in our
particular society or group. We are given gifts of discernment and
other indications that a person travels a similar road or a different one
from ourselves: I believe we're not acting with love if we know of a
smoother way and don't share it. But, in the end, the only person's
salvation we can know anything about is our own. To close the box on
any person or category of people is both to assume a knowledge that
we don't have and to deny God the freedom to be merciful and
compassionate when so moved. "Everyone who loves is born of God
and knows God." Does that put any of us out of reach? I still have my
questions about Hitler, but God's salvation certainly includes my
friend Celeste! How I wish I could have seen that when we were teens.

6

Where Two or Three Are Gathered

One of the places where it's easiest to see the way God-boxes can both help and hinder is in the practice of corporate worship. Services of worship are the basic building blocks of our churches. If a tiny church has nothing else in the way of programs or events, it still has some form of worship service, and there's an entire industry devoted to teaching us how to do it well. Those of us who have been active in church life have a ton of worship-related things in our God-boxes. They represent our likes and dislikes, our good and bad worship experiences, and our general sense of how we go about this thing called worship.

Although we often have some very strong ideas about what worship should and shouldn't look like, few individuals, and even fewer churches, have ever really sat down to think about what worship is. So before we look at the ways that we close boxes and make idols in worship, I want to look at the nature of worship itself. What is it we are doing? What is worship anyway?

Books have been written about that question alone, and I don't want to go too far down that road. But I do want to say that worship, at its heart, is simply the adoration of God. Sometimes it's public and sometimes it's private. It's the particular way that each of us, alone or corporately, expresses the depth of our love for God. I will spare you a long, scriptural defense of that definition, but suffice it to say when I look at passages in the Bible, like the stunning scenes of worship in the book of Revelation, that's what it seems to me is happening. Our love of God begins with praise and deepens into worship.

Worship Service?

Now, by that definition, much that takes place in what Protestants call a "worship service" isn't exactly worship. Worship is focused on God, while much of our service is focused on other things. Maybe if we called it the "worship and service," we'd come closer to what we're actually doing when most of us gather.

A sermon, for example, isn't really worship—it's instruction, maybe, or inspiration. It might be about God. We hope it is, although when I began seminary in Atlanta, I went to four different United Methodist churches before I heard God mentioned in a sermon. A sermon might inspire us to worship, but it isn't worship itself. It's true that, as a pastor, part of the way I express my devotion to God is by preaching God's word to God's people. So preaching could perhaps be considered an act of worship for me, but unless it's a really bad sermon, I'm not the only one in the room. For the majority, listening to my sermon isn't worship. I'm not saying it doesn't belong in a service, I'm just pointing out that we do other things besides worship when we gather.

Announcements, even those announcing worship services, aren't worship. They're helpful, and often they're an indicator of the life of a congregation, lifting up ministries vital to who we are as the Body of Christ, and sometimes spurring people to life-changing experiences. But announcements aren't worship.

Sometimes even the things designed to be worship aren't worship. If we're not careful, our prayers can cease to be worship. When pastoral prayers become sermons directed at the congregation, or when prayer is simply presenting a list of people we would like to be healed and contains no praise and thanksgiving, it's no longer worship. That doesn't make it wrong, it just makes it something else. Music can be worship, but music can also be performance. Words of praise and adoration, whether planned in a liturgy or spoken spontaneously, may or may not be worship, depending on where the heart of the speaker is focused. When it's adoration directed at God, it's worship. When it's directed toward others in the congregation or done merely as duty or obligation, it's not worship, at least from my perspective. Worship is an attitude of the heart, not an outward form.

All of this means that we shouldn't close the box and say that corporate worship is the only valid worship there is. Your grandson is not God-less simply because he will not darken a church door, and the fact that your grandmother was in church every Sunday for seventy-five years doesn't necessarily mean that she ever truly worshiped God. It would be surprising if she didn't, but it's not out of the realm of possibility.

On the flip side, I once talked with a man who took Scripture so literally that he thought the verse in Matthew 18:20—about Jesus being there when two or three were gathered—meant that it was wrong to gather more than two or three! For him, Jesus apparently left if a fourth showed up. There is a host of ways that we close the box.

Being corporate doesn't make it worship, or as the saying goes, "Sittin' in a bread basket don't make you a biscuit." When someone says she can worship God just as well in her garden, she's right. It's worship when the heart is turned in adoration toward God, regardless of whether we're alone or with others. In one sense, worship is always singular. It doesn't matter what's happening around you. You're not worshiping just because the person in front of you is. Worship has first and foremost to do with what is going on in your own heart between you and God.

That said, our own personal worship is amazingly magnified when it's combined with the worship of others. The whole becomes greater than the sum of the parts, and those who never participate in true corporate worship are missing out. You might love to make the shower tiles rattle singing "How Great Thou Art," but even your greatest shower anthem cannot compete with two hundred devoted voices doing the same thing. It changes it, somehow. Not that either style of worship—corporate or singular—is better, just that each has special joys and comforts that are not available in the other. Closing the box and saying worship can be only one way or the other diminishes our lives and our worship.

Thou Shalt Have No Other Gods

Almost every church has a history riddled with horror stories about conflicts over worship. In and of itself, conflict over worship can be a healthy thing. Wrestling with what it means to worship God in a particular community can be one of the best things a church ever does for itself. It's not conflict that causes the horror stories. It's the way we sometimes deal with conflict that results in splits and wars and the wounding of God's children.

The premise of this book is that the real harm in addressing our differences comes from closing our God-box and trying to make what is true for us into the entirety of God's truth. The biblical word for this is idolatry, and there are more idols in the typical church than anybody can list. Pastors, especially, find coming to a new church something like exploring ground filled with land mines. We know coming in that there are idols somewhere—every church has them—but we often don't know where they are until we unknowingly step on one and blow our legs off.

Generally we have some help with this in seminary, and being trained as a United Methodist, I received help with some of the idols that tend to be found in mainline Protestant churches. Tread lightly if you see a memorial plaque on something. Be even more careful if it's in the sanctuary. And if something with a plaque is sitting under the cross, tamper with it and you will surely die. By morning. The Bible says the fear of the Lord is the beginning of wisdom, but fear of church furniture can't be too far behind. Just try suggesting that you replace the pews with chairs. A seat is a seat, you reason. You would be wrong.

If you still have your legs after replacing the pews, you might be tempted to head toward the music. Nobody should get through seminary these days without recognizing that many, many churches have become shrines for the god *Organus Pipus*. I love the organ myself, and if you can crank it up and rattle the windows with it, so much the better. I always thought it was one of many great instruments. Silly me. How was I to know it was an instrument that descended directly from heaven into the church sanctuary? Somewhere I missed the Bible verse that says it is the only instrument allowed in worship. Stray from its keyboard at your peril. But more on that later.

My point is that worship is full of idols: individual or corporate God-boxes that have been closed off and identified as the only legitimate form of worship. Generally, the new pastor is the most obvious victim of the idol's wrath. In some churches, we get toasted for changing the order of worship. In others, we can set a congregation back ten years merely by moving the service time fifteen minutes one way or the other. And almost every congregation will feel out of sorts if we change anything at all about Communion. And how long should a worship service be? Apparently in many places our devotion is so emotionally charged and intense that God cannot bear more than an hour of it. Preference is not a problem. Idolatry is.

So If We Just Get Rid of the Pews . . .

Because of all of that, a number of pastors and church leaders have gone to the opposite extreme and have begun to close off their boxes to anything that smacks of tradition. The nontraditional person running headlong into a closed-tradition box is likely to hear the thunderous chant, "We've never done it that way before." When someone encounters such a tradition-bound congregation, an equal and opposite reaction can occur: a closed, nontraditional box.

Pastors and congregations burned one time too many by traditions that have become idols have been known to respond with an idol of their own: no traditions at all. There's no room for the traditions of the church in these services at all. Tradition becomes as forbidden in worship as the nontraditional is in other places.

I ran headlong into such a nontraditional box at a church where I had the delightful task of creating a new worship service from the ground up. I could schedule it for any day at any hour for any length of time. It didn't have to look like the other services and there were no preset rules—no idols to wrestle before I could begin. At least that's what I thought.

But what they really meant, as it turned out, was something else. I was free to dispense with tradition, but my troubles came when I wanted to include traditions, especially weekly Communion. As the shape of the service began to emerge, I found myself battering the lid of a new box that I had never really thought about before. In this situation, tradition wasn't a god, it was a devil, and that devil was as unwelcome, at least to church leadership, as the devil normally is in church circles.

It's not that my friends and colleagues were trying to be mean or difficult. They had a true heart for the unchurched and voiced their concerns out of love for those who might not feel welcome if they were surrounded by traditions that they couldn't understand. For my part, I felt that someone coming to church for the first time should have glimpses of mystery. But we never could come to agreement. My particular form for the service may or may not have been a good one; that's not the issue. The issue is deciding that God can be present in some things and not in others.

I've come down hard on some mainline idols, but other traditions aren't exempt. For a good number of years, I assumed it was impossible for God to be present in a church with a printed bulletin. Prayers read off of a page couldn't possibly reach the heart of God, and if I heard one more responsive reading, I thought I would run from the room screaming. Because God didn't touch me through those things, I came to believe God could touch no one that way. I was wrong, not only about God's ability to use liturgy and order in the lives of others, but about the possibility that God would one day speak to me in exactly those ways.

As a pastor, I've run into the nontraditional box in my approach to sermons. I preach from a manuscript and, most of the time, do it from behind the pulpit. No matter that people say they love my sermons, no matter that I've won awards for preaching, no matter that God manages to work through my preaching to change lives. For some, I'm just doing it wrong. I should be free from the manuscript and out from behind the pulpit.

I remember a man who began visiting my first church with his girl-friend. He was from an Assemblies of God tradition, and he spoke to me one day about my use of a manuscript. I should get rid of it, he said, and let God speak through me. Didn't I trust the Holy Spirit to give me the words? Well, I didn't change. After a couple of months, tragedy struck and the man ended up convicted of a crime and sent to a California prison. I got a letter from him. It seems his girlfriend had been copying my sermons (I always left a copy by the copy machine so the hard of hearing could read along) and sending them to him in prison. He was getting so much from them that he had begun circu-lating them to many other inmates, and he was glad I'd never taken his advice to abandon the manuscript. I still believe that the Holy Spirit can inspire preparation as well as spontaneity.

And while we're on the Holy Spirit side of the street, let's talk a bit about tongues. As I mentioned earlier, I spent a fair amount of time as a devoted fan of the Assemblies of God and charismatic worship. I still enjoy that free style to this day. I also speak in tongues and, while I have never felt moved to give a prophecy or other public utterance in a tongue, I do find it to be a wonderful gift in prayer.

When my heart is so full of joy or sorrow or some other over-whelming emotion, there simply is no English expression that can say what needs to be said. In those times, I don't even know what needs to be said. All I know is that my heart is bursting or breaking. I need to speak something aloud, to communicate somehow with the God who made and loves me. But there are no words. In those moments, speaking in tongues fills the void. Whether it is actually a language from another part of the globe, a heavenly language, or pure babble doesn't much matter to me. I know that as I speak, God can hear my heart. My need to give voice to my joy or pain is met, and I am confident that God understands. I have no issues with the general practice of speaking in tongues.

I do, however, have issues with theologies that close the box: either to say that without the gift of tongues the Holy Spirit cannot be present or to deny God's presence in the gift. Whatever happened to "the wind blows where it chooses" (John 3:8)? I know it goes on to say that you "hear the sound of it," but does the sound have to be unintelligible? Many times in Scripture we read about the presence of the Holy Spirit being made manifest through tongues, and especially with the new Gentile converts, such signs were probably essential to their eventual acceptance by the Jewish Christians in Jerusalem. There are times when such things are necessary for some to see the work of God as valid. But there is a difference between saying that it is *a* sign and it is *the only* sign. I'm not aware that Jesus spoke in tongues.

It seems just as silly to me to say that tongues are no longer a valid expression of the Spirit. Says who? If you're referring to St. Paul's words that "as for tongues, they will cease," in 1 Corinthians 13:8, are you really prepared to say that the time he meant is now? Is knowledge also gone? Is prophecy gone? I will grant that the practice of tongues can and does get out of hand in some places. I think that 1 Corinthians 14 should be preached at least once a year in charismatic churches, for it provides some necessary correctives. But I hardly think that closing the box and declaring the practice invalid is called for.

It doesn't matter whether we are pronouncing anathema on the organ or the tambourine, tongues or ordered speech, pews or chairs. Both traditional and nontraditional approaches, I think, are idols: attempts to control the way God can and cannot be present in worship. "The LORD does not see as mortals see; they look on the outward appearance, but the LORD looks on the heart" (1 Sam 16:7).

I think we could all be a lot happier if we would quit closing our boxes. Traditions will neither ensure nor prevent the presence of God in your church. God happens to be a free agent. In Scripture, God both prescribes elaborate traditions and rituals and expresses hatred and disdain for them, depending not on the ritual but on the heart with which they are engaged. I think if we can remember this, we will find the road to meaningful worship a lot smoother.

Many Gifts, One Spirit

Worship will not, however, be conflict-free. We are different people. When we're at home, we like to eat different foods and listen to different music. We work at different jobs, have quite different ideas about what constitutes "fun," and become friends with or even marry folks that other people wouldn't touch with a ten-foot pole. So why is it that we expect, when it comes to a church service, that we will all suddenly be of one mind about what is "good" music, whether liturgy should be prepared or spontaneous, or whether we would like to kneel, sit, or stand during Communion?

Let's go back to *Organus Pipus* for a minute. I'm not here to tell anybody that they should give up liking organ music. But organs did not suddenly appear in churches around the globe by some divine miracle. Organs weren't manna that fell from the sky, and they caused as much of a stir when they were first introduced from the secular world into the church as the guitar and drums have done in more recent times. There's nothing at all wrong with saying, "I prefer the organ in church." The problem is in saying that we're not having worship if the organ doesn't play—that somehow God isn't pleased with other instruments or with no instruments at all.

The same goes for other stylistic differences in worship. Do we use hymnals or song sheets or do we project the words on a screen on the wall? Do we recite a creed and, if so, which one? How do we involve children in worship? Should people be free to speak out during prayer? To lift their hands? To dance? How do we determine what happens when? How many services should we have and when should they be? Our answers to all of that and more will be as different as we are.

All of those things and many others are important and need to be sorted through according to the life and mission of a given congregation. I don't mean to imply that they're immaterial. As your church does the hard work of hashing out what it means to worship God in your congregation in your region, you may decide that, for instance, you'll use certain traditions sparingly or not at all. Or you may decide that the people both inside and outside the church are so located in history and tradition that very traditional worship works best. Every congregation will put some things and not others in their box. The only edict is this: don't close the box. Recognize that *your* way of worship isn't the sum total of worship itself.

Until we can recognize that holiness is intrinsic to the heart and not the form, our discussion over our differences will tear us apart. There's nothing at all the matter with looking in our own God-box and saying, "You know, guitars are just not going to fit in there. I just don't like them." The problem comes when we insist that because guitars won't fit in our box, that it's wrong for others to have them in theirs. It's also a problem for those of us with open boxes to say that it's wrong for others to look at their box and say, "You know, an organ just won't go in there. Been there. Done that. It doesn't fit." It is not wrong to prefer one thing over another or to acknowledge that God moves you in this way and not that. The problem comes in making our own preferences the boundary for how God can work in all lives, at all times, and in all places.

If we close the box, we've also closed the door to those who might otherwise like to come in. The act of worship doesn't somehow erase our personality and our tastes, and yet that's what we often signal to the world outside our doors. If country music is the style of music that moves my soul, why would I turn to the organ to express my soul's greatest joy in God? In some places it could be that the dwindling number of people in worship simply reflects the dwindling number of people who love organ music.

Do you want to reach out to others? Others who might like different things? Every congregation will have to decide that for itself, and it's beyond my scope here to talk about how a church goes about that difficult but critical process. My job is simply to point out that the state of your God-box is related to the question, and if your box is closed, chances are your church doors will be also.

Our life together in Christian community can only be tolerable to the extent that we can contain our urge to close the box, but that's not to say that we don't make choices about what will go into our box at any given point in time. We can be selective without being closed. Individuals have to discover the keys to unlocking worship for them-selves. As we do that, we put those things in our God-box. Ideally, we don't close it up and disallow new experiences or think that our prefer-ences are right for everyone, but we do have things that are in and things that are out of our box.

Those things represent the unique combination of gifts and interests that we bring to a larger group. What we bring to share, like a potluck dinner, should enhance the experience for everyone, making the God-box of our community larger and more diverse. That's what the whole notion of the Body of Christ is about. What we seek is unity, not uniformity. "If the whole body were an eye, where would the hearing be? If the whole body were hearing, where would the sense of smell be (1 Cor 12:17)?"

In the same way, our local congregation develops (with much prayer) a God-box, an identity that is open to expansion and change, but one that is still making constant decisions about what will or won't go in its particular box at present. Those congregational boxes then represent the unique offering that they bring to their denomination, if they are part of one, or to other faith communities in their area. The image of the Body of Christ with different functions and gifts works, I think, for groups as well as for individuals.

Suppose we quit looking at other churches suspiciously. Suppose we quit closing the box and remained open to the way God is being made manifest in other places? Suppose the different gifts of the Body of Christ weren't just divided among individuals like Margaret and Steven and Sue, but were also divided among Baptists and Presbyterians, Episcopalians and Roman Catholics? I think each tradition has something to offer the larger God-box of humanity.

My own life has been a mix of many Christian traditions. I began American Baptist. By my teens, I was moonlighting at an Assembly of God church and went to a Roman Catholic prayer meeting on Tuesday nights. In college, I was a Presbyterian. When I moved to Maryland, I became a Southern Baptist and then a United Methodist, and from time to time, through all of it, have gone to Mass with my Catholic grandmother or with other friends and have visited in many other churches. I find that they have all helped me to grow. They are all different and have different ways of focusing faith. My faith today is more balanced because of the gifts each gave to me.

From the American Baptist box I took a love of the Bible. The Assemblies taught me that worship could be fun and free and wild, while the Catholic Church reminded me that there was a place for holy silence. The Presbyterians reminded me that God had a plan for my life, and the Methodists reminded me that I could accept it or not as I chose. The Southern Baptists reminded me that the character of my personal life was important, while the Methodists balanced that with a commitment to social justice. Baptists gave me obedience; Catholics, Episcopalians, and Methodists gave me sacrament. Presbyterians gave me the sovereignty of God; the Assemblies gave me a friend in Jesus; Episcopalians showed me that liturgy can bring order out of chaos, while Quakers reminded me that sometimes pure silence is best. Protestants gave me a God I could understand and approach, the Catholics reminded me of God's mystery, Orthodox churches connected me with the communion of saints.

I could go on and on, but the point is that all of those traditions together have been the Body of Christ for me. Each has brought a unique gift to my faith and I feel more balanced and at peace in my spiritual skin because of it. But I couldn't get that if I closed the box. If I close myself to Southern Baptist or Roman Catholic witness simply because they close themselves to mine as a woman pastor, I have lost out. Because I disagree with some things or ultimately choose to worship with a different community doesn't mean that there's nothing for me to learn from the others.

The same is true even with other faiths. Believing the truth of the Christian witness doesn't prevent me from finding any truth in Islam or Buddhism. I've often thought that the spread of Buddhism in the materialistic West may well be just what the doctor ordered to try to put the brakes on our unbounded greed: even the church is too infected with the disease to do much to halt it. Eugene Peterson, in his book *Leap over a Wall,* describes "a public Christian identity dominated by bumper-sticker labels and television celebrities that nurture in people an insatiable appetite for watching religious performance and an indiscriminate eagerness for buying junk religious artifacts."[3] And that comes from a fellow Christian. While the church remains neurotically focused on sexuality, deadly avarice is worming its way into our hearts, just as it already rules the heart of the culture around us.

When we realize that our national sin is greed, the church can be right there (first in the repentance line) with the truth of God's grace and forgiveness. In the meantime, however, it may well take the Buddhists to turn the corner for us. They remind us that our suffering comes from our inordinate desires, and that the way to God comes

---

3. Eugene Peterson, *Leap over a Wall: Earthly Spirituality for Everyday Christians* (New York: Harper San Francisco, 1998), 18.

through giving up our attachment to having life the way we want it. They offer to us the truth that getting caught up in our passions can lead to suffering and death. We bring to them the paradox of embracing suffering and death—the cross—as a way to freedom. I once met a man who had recently converted to Christianity. "I could never have become a Christian without first being a Buddhist," he claimed. "The Buddhists taught me to live with paradox." It may take the Neo-Pagans and the Native Americans together to get us to quit assaulting the earth. Let's not close the box and say they have nothing to offer to our faith.

Theory of Relativity

I'm not advocating total relativism—that the only things that are true are those things that are true for me. I do believe in the existence of absolute truth, but I just don't believe we can be certain of what it is. I believe the nature of truth is rather like the nature of infinity: we can get closer to it than we currently are, but we can't ever arrive. The number 1,542 is closer to infinity than the number 9, but we can get closer still than 1,542. In fact, whatever number we come up with can always be increased by adding one more. If we closed off the box and said, "There. No more numbers after this one," we would have deluded ourselves, and I think that ultimately our delusions harm us.

To say that we can't name a number that is infinity isn't to say there's no such thing as infinity; it merely expresses our limitations in understanding. So it is, I believe, with the truth of God. I'm not saying there is no absolute truth. But in our mortal state, we can't know what it is. What we can do—what humility dictates we must do—is to admit that there can always be higher numbers than the ones we currently know. We can know that we have progressed from 5 to 5,000 and know we're headed in the right direction, but we also know that 5,000 is not the last word. Infinity is bigger than any human number and God is bigger than any human truth.

In worship, we must remember that we're not God. Our form of worship is not God. The closer our worship can come to expressing the breadth of God's nature, the more effective our witness will be, and for that reason we are wise to be thoughtful and purposeful in our worship planning and design. But, ultimately, our planning and design cannot of themselves invoke God or prevent God from being present in our midst. When a child of God shows up for worship, God is there, even if that child is not dressed properly.

The attitude for which I praise God is the attitude of an older woman in one of the congregations I served. I'll call her Betty. Betty is, at heart, a traditionalist. If she went strictly with her preferences, she'd come to the 10:30 traditional service, would hear only the organ, and would enjoy the quiet and orderly reverence of that form of worship. But Betty has a neighbor we'll call Becky, who is nine years old. Becky's family doesn't go to church, but Becky wants to come and go to Sunday school. Sunday school meets during the first service at 9 a.m.

Betty doesn't really like the nine o'clock service. It's too noisy with all the children, and the liturgy in the first part doesn't flow as smoothly because the children do it rather than the adults who are liturgists at second service. The music is provided by a guitar and drum band, and many of Betty's beloved traditional elements are missing. We don't sing the Gloria or recite a creed or have a separate prayer of confession at the nine o'clock service, but Betty now faithfully attends it so that she can give God to her little neighbor. Becky loves that first service. She loves the upbeat music, the chance to lead worship, the children's message, and the chance to learn about God in Sunday school. Betty has decided that the mission of the church is about sharing God with others rather than with indulging our own preferences.

Betty hasn't dispensed with her box, but neither has she closed the lid. She's tried not to force Becky to like what she likes, because Betty no longer believes (if she ever did) that her preferences in worship were a divine mandate. The only real mandate she now hears is "Go and make disciples." Oh, for a church full of Bettys! People's preferences shouldn't be ignored. That is why many churches with more than one worship service try to have services that reflect different styles and tastes. It's not easy to help both Betty and Becky find a home under one roof. Such a union is only possible if, like Betty, we keep the lid off of our boxes.

7

Who Is on the Lord's Side?

Many of the world's atrocities have been committed with the perpetrators' full conviction that God is on their side. While not every issue I mention is in league with atrocity, that's a predictable end when certain personalities are combined with closed God-boxes.

Maybe we're always a little more comfortable with certainty than with doubt, but it would have been helpful if Hitler had some doubts about racial supremacy, if the Inquisitors hadn't been quite so sure what constituted heresy, if the Crusaders had left room for even a bit of fidelity in the "infidel." How might history have been different if we were a little less willing to believe that we had God completely figured out and God's will completely mastered? Yet we continue, on both the conservative and liberal ends of the spectrum, to equate our cause with God's and to proclaim the other side unfit for the kingdom. In the end, we're all diminished.

In this chapter I want to look at what I believe to be some dangerous roads that we currently travel, in the hopes that we can keep those roads from becoming a trail of tears. Again let me emphasize that I write these things as my public confession and repentance for living in such ways myself. In my teens and early twenties I was a staunch conservative and about as intolerant as they come, at least in religious matters. When the lessons of Scripture, mixed with the lessons of life, blew apart that box, I swung to the opposite extreme and could tolerate anything but intolerance, merely swapping the residents of heaven and hell like the changing sands in an hourglass. Neither position brought peace.

So I bring to you here the view from both sides, not to create a new intolerance for anything but the middle ground, but rather to promote a new openness for the parts of truth that each side holds. God is, in some sense, on all sides. To paraphrase Psalm 139, "Where can I go from your spirit? Or where can I flee from your presence? If I move to the right you are there; if I pitch my tent with the liberals, you are there. If I preach the evils of evolution on Darwin's grave or travel to the Red Sea to claim it never parted, even there your hand shall lead me, and your right hand shall hold me fast."

We can't trap God in a single ideology, social agenda, or political platform. Maybe if we could remember that, we wouldn't be so tempted to demonize the other side. Pro-choice people don't want to kill babies, and pro-lifers don't hate women. Democrats don't want to shirk responsibility and let the government do it for them, and Republicans do in fact have compassion for the poor. It's bad enough that we squabble and call people names like children, but do we have to drag God into the fray? Mixing God into our already volatile language only brings us the death of abortion doctors, the deeds of Timothy McVeigh, and war.

Church and State

Let's look at religion and politics for a minute. It's not a given that Christians will vote with one mind on election day. It's also not true that those Christians who voted differently than you did are necessarily misguided or have less faith. Good, solid Christian folks can be found behind every candidate and on both sides of every issue, and many of them have specifically made that choice in a spirit of prayer and a desire to do God's will.

Suppose we look at the Conservative/Liberal polarity in the Christian faith as simply the two pieces of the Great Commandment. The beauty of fundamentalism, at least for me, is its devotion. The Christian Right hasn't forgotten the first part of the Great Commandment: "You shall love the Lord your God with all your heart, and with all your soul, and with all your mind, and with all your strength." Faith, if it's the sort of faith the Bible teaches, affects every single part of your life during every minute that you draw breath and beyond. All people of faith will not vote the same way, and some people's faith may dictate that they do not vote at all, but no one fully living out the first part of the Great Commandment can say that faith has no effect on their political stand. You might as well say that I will have faith all the time except Tuesdays and Thursdays after dinner. The commandment says "all . . . all . . . all . . . all" and fundamentalism has that part exactly right. Jesus looked to his faith when paying taxes (Matt 17:27), when confronted with a decision on capital punishment (John 8:1–11), and when deciding to engage in civil disobedience (Matt 12:1–8). As with everything else, the problem isn't so much bringing God into the issue at hand, as binding God to and even equating God with the particular side we've chosen to support. The problem is not having the box, but closing it.

For the view from the left, the beauty of liberalism is compassion. Their standard bears the picture of Jesus feeding the hungry, healing the sick, eating with sinners, rampaging through the temple in righteous indignation over the trampling of the poor. Liberalism is the advocate for the second part of the Great Commandment: "Love your neighbor as yourself." The liberal camp reminds us that while issues of personal morality may grab our attention, there's a social dimension to morality that can't be ignored if we take our faith seriously. Just consider Jesus' admonitions in Matthew 25:31–46 to feed the hungry and clothe the naked.

Liberals remind us that budget decisions and trade agreements and health-care provisions are as much moral choices as abortion and marital fidelity, and that sin is often so much a part of the systems in which we live that individual moral choices are sometimes not even possible. Liberals remind us that the heart of Jesus' message often got through to society's outcasts before it reached the religious establishment.

I believe that we need both sets of voices for balance, and I believe that so strongly that it is how I vote. By ideology, I am a Democrat. But I want the White House and Congress to represent different parties. Each voice needs to be heard and each voice needs political clout. While I can't swallow the doctrine of original sin whole, enough of it rings true that I'm afraid to have no brakes on the train in the political arena. I just can't let go and trust that sin won't find its way into our political system. If one party controls both Congress and the White House, its own shortcomings will multiply, unchecked. Each side, I believe, needs the wisdom of the other. My solution to the 2000 election debacle in the United States was to elect both Bush and Gore. Put two desks in the Oval Office, give them both veto power, and let Congress come up with bills that only both of them could sign. So we might only get one bill signed in four years: at least it would be a good one. We've got to come to grips with the fact that the people in the pews around us have voted in all sorts of ways, many of which we find offensive. But we can be sure of this: their voting habits haven't expelled them from the Kingdom of God.

Humble Pie

Don't think I'm saying it doesn't really matter how we vote or where we stand on issues. Once again, it's the difference between having a box and closing the lid on it. We rightly make decisions about what does and doesn't belong in our God-box. According to God's leading, we decide between right and wrong. What I call leaving the box open is simply asking for some humility as we make our decisions. That means that I recognize in my humanity that I may have right and wrong mixed up to some degree. So may others. We are all in this human project together, trying to find our way through with integrity.

When I was appointed to my first church in rural Florida, the issue of a woman in the pulpit was a big one and needed to be addressed. I set aside my first Sunday night there as a time when I would share my faith journey with the congregation and allow them to ask whatever questions they wanted of me. The sanctuary was packed. I suppose there must have been friendly faces, but what I saw were arms crossed over chests and very dour, determined looks.

So I began to tell my story. I shared my call to ministry at the age of fourteen and my own scriptural struggles with whether I, as a woman, belonged in a pastoral position. I told of all the other ways that I tried to fit into church life, doing everything from acting as Sunday school superintendent to serving as choir director to painting the walls.

"But in the end," I said, "God kept putting me back at the helm, blessing me when I did what pastors do. I may be completely wrong in assuming I should be here, but at least grant me that I am very sincerely wrong. I have prayed and struggled and wrestled with the will of God for my life, and in going into the pastoral ministry am simply doing what I believe God has called me to do. If you have determined that is wrong, please pray for me, but for now I am doing all I know to do."

I finished my piece and opened up for questions, holding my breath in the initial silence. A woman at the back stood up and said, "I think we should all sing 'Trust and Obey' because that's what Anne has done." I love that woman. I doubt that we have ever voted for the same candidate or have ever been on the same side of a social issue, but that didn't keep the spirit of God from living and working within both of us that night. The dam was broken with her words, people openly told me of changed minds, and I was able to minister in that congregation from that night forward.

We all came into that room knowing we were on different sides. We had made different decisions about what was right and what was wrong. But because we were each able to leave room for integrity of faith on the other side, we were able to worship and minister together under one roof. And that's the point. Leave room for your own errors in judgment, and leave room for sincerity of faith in those who have decided differently. Or as the saying goes, "Make your words sweet; you might have to eat them."

This is why diversity in a congregation is so important to our spiritual health. We can't keep a diverse congregation under the same roof without humility, and it's the challenges brought by that diversity that can give us the humility we need. We might start with diversity, but without humility, our differences will soon lead to fractions and splits. Those who don't share the mind of the majority will leave to find a more comfortable place. Those who are left might think that it's all worked out for the best—that the infidel has left and the faithful remain. But what's happened, in fact, is that all sides have moved further from the Kingdom of God.

This Train Is Bound for Glory

I haven't heard that heaven's neighborhoods are going to be segregated according to political and social ideology. So I figure that if I'm going to find heaven at all heavenly, I'd better learn to like the diversity here. That doesn't mean I can't decide to reject certain positions. It simply means that I can't decide to reject the faith of the people who disagree.

For instance, at this stage in my faith, I take a very open stand on all the religious issues surrounding homosexuality. That hasn't always been the case, and what I once defended (even in print) as "right," I now believe to be "wrong." In looking at the way my own faith has moved (and homosexuality is not the only issue on which I've done an about-face), I find the truth of Jesus' words that in judging others we only judge ourselves. I can say at this point that I think closing the lid to exclude the gifts of those of homosexual orientation is harmful. But I can't say that those who do decide to close the lid aren't Christian or have no faith, without saying that at the point in my life when I did the same I had no faith either. To judge their faith is to judge my own. And I know better. I know I had faith then just as I do now.

Faith is about our relationship with God, and like any relationship we can make good and bad decisions from within it. If a teenager goes out, gets drunk, and wrecks the car, I can look at that and say she made some bad choices. But it would be silly for me to determine from that action that she had no relationship with her parents or that her parents were unfit. For good or for ill, we're free agents, and being in a good relationship doesn't preclude our making bad choices. In the same way, we can't say that people aren't in relationship with God because they've made a choice we believe to be wrong. In my own case, knowing how my notions of "right" and "wrong" have shifted over time, I'd be condemning either my past or my future faith.

I've seen in my life that the citizens of both heaven and hell have never been able to unpack, because I keep moving them from one place to the other. Finally, I've seen how silly that is. If we can recognize that people of faith can hold positions we consider to be "wrong," I think we're well poised to renew the church. When we make social, political, and moral agendas into marks that can unswervingly identify a Christian, I think we've lost our true center.

Seek Ye First the Kingdom of God

I think that's exactly what the church, in both its conservative and liberal manifestations, has done. We've lost our center, or at least we've come dangerously close. The center of the Christian church is the revelation of God in Jesus Christ.

The liberal branch of the church has often flirted with making social justice issues the center. I hear terms like the "preferential option for the poor" with bewilderment. Certainly God often, if not always, champions the poor. God must do this, since we human beings often, if not always, refuse to hear their cause. But does God really "prefer" the poor? Is being poor a badge of holiness? Did Jesus always shun the rich? Not in my Bible. In fact, just before the "love your neighbor as yourself" passage in Leviticus 19:18, we read the words, "You shall not render an unjust judgment; you shall not be partial to the poor or defer to the great: with justice you shall judge your neighbor" (Lev 19:15). The point is to be impartial, not to swap out who receives all the attention.

The liberal voice is absolutely right to advocate for those who have no voice and to remind us all that the call to peace with justice is a critical part of the Christian vocation. Think Sodom and Gomorrah were destroyed because of homosexuality? Read Ezekiel 16:49: "This was the guilt of your sister Sodom: she and her daughters had pride, excess of food, and prosperous ease, but did not aid the poor and needy." We need to be confronted with this message always. Justice concerns flow naturally from our center in Christ, but they are not the center itself.

Paradoxically, I think moving justice to the center removes justice. If justice is the center of our faith, we have no message of salvation to bring to the unjust. We can no longer be fair and impartial. We can only condemn. Works, not faith, occupy center stage. With justice at the center, Jesus can no longer decide to eat with—and save— Zacchaeus, the rich tax collector who spent his life defrauding the poor (Luke 19:1–10). With justice at the center we can't bear Jesus' words to the thief on the cross: "Today you will be with me in Paradise" (Luke 23:39–43). Taking justice from the center, of course, doesn't mean moving it to the back. We're so prone to polar thinking that it's desperately hard to show that issues can be vitally important without being at the center. But the center of our faith is a person, not an issue.

To those on the right, it needs to be said that the center is not doctrine, either as it's expressed in the biblical witness or in the creeds and traditions of the church. We're saved by entering into a loving relationship with the living God, not by assenting to the correct doctrine. Our center is a living being, not a creed. It is not the Bible, but the One whom the Bible reveals that we worship. When conservatives lose their center, this is most generally the form that it takes: Protestant conservatives tend to put the Bible at the center, while Catholic and Orthodox conservatives tend to reserve the space for creeds and tradition. Now I don't want conservatives going polar on me either. I'm not relegating these things to the trash heap. As with justice issues, I merely want to dethrone them as idols in order to give God the honored place.

Let's take the issue of praying to the saints as an example. I've had faithful Protestants come to me concerned for the salvation of their Catholic family and friends because they pray to the Virgin Mary and to the saints. But the question could just as easily have come from a Catholic concerned about a friend's seeming idolatry of the Bible. Putting either the Bible or doctrine at the center is a problem. If I pray to the wrong thing, I could be in trouble.

But with God in the center, there's a little more breathing room. If I put in a sincere call to the heavenly switchboard, God will lovingly understand any confusion and wrong numbers that I might have and forward my call to the right person. It might be that no matter whose extension you dial, you get God anyway; or it might be that all direct calls to God get routed to whatever saint is free at the moment. With God at the center, we have the simple assurance that our sincere prayer is heard with love. How that works, exactly, makes little difference. We can have our prayers answered all the same.

With God at the center we're free to examine and refine our doctrines and creeds so that they more truly reflect the God we proclaim. With a doctrine or creed in the center, a request for examination or reformation becomes heresy. Likewise with the Bible. Remove it from the center and we can be open to new interpretation or even, as the apostles were in Acts 15, new covenants. Build the faith around it, however, and it becomes an agent of suppression.

I Serve a Risen Savior

This is why the doctrine of the resurrection of Jesus is so important. As a doctrine, it can't go in the center. Yes, people of real faith can question or even deny a real resurrection. But what we believe about the resurrection is vitally important in helping us to know our center. If the center is a good, but very dead, teacher, that's quite a different matter from a living and eternal God, and it will affect our lives in very different ways. If the center is an abstract symbol of the cycle of death and life, that will bring out a different response than a relationship with a personal and resurrected Jesus.

All that is to say that our doctrine, which I believe needs to be formed in conversation with the Bible, is critically important. It determines whether I feel comfortable or frightened when I pray. It determines if I even will pray in the first place. It structures many of the details of my life in faith. But if any of it—doctrine, creed, or Bible—sits in the center, we've all denied the resurrection, for we are worshiping something dead rather than someone alive.

Idols of these sorts are, it must be said, comfortable. However many difficulties there are in putting the Bible, a creed, or a particular issue in the center, we at least know where those things begin and end. They can be contained and they'll stay where we put them. A God who won't stay in his tomb is most annoying. First he appears here, then there. One minute he's eating fish and the next he's walking through walls. You can never really be sure where he's going to be or what he's going to be up to. Which is exactly the point of this book. Try if you like to seal the tomb, but he'll simply put the guards to sleep, blow the stone from the door, and walk out. I've put it in terms of blowing the lid off the God-box, but the New Testament puts it more simply: "He is not here, but has risen" (Luke 24:5). Jesus is on the loose.

I think that our penchant for idolatry is why many churches find themselves in decline. The answer is not a new program or a new pastor or a new building. The answer is resurrection. We need to quit worshiping something dead and look to the living God. As Scripture says, "It is a fearful thing to fall into the hands of the living God." Of course it is. God, by definition, is in charge. God is the one with the power and the glory forever and ever. We can't control God; if we could, the word "God" would have no meaning. All of that is fearsome enough: which of us likes the idea of not being in control of what happens to us? But a living God? Eeek. We like gods who will stay in shrines where we put them, not living deities that wander about doing things we haven't authorized.

And yet it's our proclamation that taking the fearsome leap of faith, which throws our lives into the hands of a living God like it was the safest thing in the world to do, is exactly what saves us. "For those who want to save their life will lose it, and those who lose their life for my sake will save it" (Luke 9:24). It is by giving up control of our lives that we gain the desire of our hearts. Paradoxical, but true. But that still doesn't mean that God will stay put. God will visit our box, even dwell in our box, but God will not be confined to it, or to anything else. When we think we have God captured, we'll discover that the only thing we've captured is a dead idol. It may be a pretty idol. It may be something holy that God has blessed. But if we confuse it with God and give our lives to its direction, we've broken the second commandment. We've closed the box, and we've substituted a dead idol for the real McCoy.

The Old, Old Story

I think that the issues in this chapter may be part of the reason that so many Christians have trouble with the Hebrew Scriptures, what we have come to call the Old Testament (as if it somehow no longer applied today). The God of the Hebrew Scriptures is very much alive and out of the box.

This is a God who cares how many loops are in the tabernacle curtains and who hears the misery of Egyptian slaves; a God who will open the earth and swallow thousands who have fallen into idolatry as well as the God who exalts the murderous, adulterous king David. It is a God who is at once particular and all-encompassing, and a God who apparently would like to keep all the apples for himself. Just as soon as we have God pegged for wrath, God is merciful; and just as soon as we think Israel can do no wrong, the temple lies in ruins and the Israelites are marched off to Babylon. We see God, as Moses did, only from the backside.

Liberals often take issue with God's seeming intolerance and wrath in these books. It doesn't matter that the Canaanite religion was rife with child sacrifice and cult prostitution, that doesn't give God license to order its obliteration. God in the Hebrew Scriptures has more patience and grace than I could ever dream of having, but this God definitely has limits. This is not a doormat God. When the Israelites in the Sinai wilderness whine one time too many, God sends poisonous snakes to shut them up. Sin too often and too long and you can expect a foreign nation to march in and sack your city.

This is disconcerting. In an age where we are committed to ending child abuse (at least in theory), it's hard to hear the story of Abraham's sacrifice of Isaac, even though he never actually goes through with the deed. In a time when we're faced with the gut-wrenching plight of the Palestinians, the biblical vendetta against the Philistines gives us pause. To modern ears, the God of the Hebrew Scriptures often seems, well, immoral and harsh.

There's no doubt that we must wrestle with these issues, but whether peace can be made is often a matter of what we've put at the center of our faith. If justice issues are at the center, I don't think there's much hope of resolution. God simply doesn't always act within the parameters we set, and if those parameters determine good and evil, well, either God is evil or this isn't the revelation of God. If a living God is at the center, we still wrestle. But even if we come up wounded in the morning, we still, like Jacob, ask for God's blessing. The questions are the same, but they're asked in the context of loving relationship, rather than in the context of suspicion.

If it hasn't been issues but rather doctrine that's become our center, we're also likely to cast off this portion of Scripture. It's the "Old" Testament, after all, and we now have a "New" one to take its place. We might want its support for our arguments in favor of capital punishment, against homosexuality, or because it so nicely lists our moral code in commandments we can hang on a wall. But in general, once we've told the standard stories to our children in Sunday school, it won't be mentioned again. It's obsolete. I actually heard pastors in seminary say that they'd never preach from the Old Testament. At best, we will read it as some sort of coded version of the New Testament; at worst we won't read it at all.

Again, as Christians we need to wrestle with the question of how these two segments of God's revelation relate to each other. If we believe that Jesus is, as John proclaims, "the Word . . . made flesh," (KJV John 1:14) just what word is it that we think became that flesh? I think it was the same word that became the Hebrew Scriptures, which was the same word of God that created all that is. It's as if God keeps trying different media to find one that will get through. God spoke and the world was created: the gift and grace of God for all to see. But we didn't see it. So God spoke again to Moses a little more plainly and encouraged him to write it down. We began to take notice, but there was still a lot of confusion. So God finally tried the word made flesh. God decided to show up in person to live out the message. And then we wrote that down, although there was perhaps less need to write it as there was to live it. We already had the written version.

Not that all of the Hebrew Scriptures were written as a prophecy of Jesus, but rather that Jesus embodied everything that God was trying to say and do in the sprawling history of God's people thus far. Rather than "Old" and "New" Testaments, we might better talk about "unabridged" and "abridged" versions, with the New Testament being more concise: just the nuts and bolts, the essentials, in the plain language of a teacher telling stories and a preacher practicing what he preached.

I've mentioned the Great Commandment a number of times. When one of the Pharisees asks Jesus which is the greatest commandment (Matt 22:34–40) Jesus answers by combining two passages from the Hebrew Scriptures: "You shall love the LORD your God with all your heart, and with all your soul, and with all your mind" from Deuteronomy 6:5 and "You shall love your neighbor as yourself" from Leviticus 19:18. He then sums up the Hebrew Scriptures by saying, "On these two commandments hang all the law and the prophets." What Jesus came to teach is rooted firmly in the Hebrew Scriptures.

When we seek to understand the Hebrew Scriptures in terms of Jesus, I think we have gone about things backwards. Our greatest benefit comes in understanding Jesus in terms of the Hebrew Scriptures. Until we can face the story of Abraham laying his only son on the altar of sacrifice, how will we face the cross? Until we come to grips with the poisonous snakes that God sent to Israel in the wilderness and the weird bronze snake that Moses put on a pole (Num 21:1–9), how will we look on the one we've pierced for our salvation? For the Christian, Jesus doesn't just come out of the context of the Hebrew Scriptures. In one sense Jesus *is* the Hebrew Scriptures: the same word made flesh. Read the book or watch the movie: same story, different medium. To reject one story is to reject the other.

In the spirit of open boxes, I don't mean to say that Jesus is *only* the Hebrew Scriptures made flesh; God's word is bigger than that. I also don't mean to say that all that might be revealed of God is revealed in the Hebrew Scriptures. I don't believe that God's revelation quit with Malachi anymore than I believe it quit with the book of Revelation, and I certainly don't believe that the enormity of God can be contained in matter, be it book or flesh. But I do believe that the basic understanding needed for salvation was laid out plainly by the end of Deuteronomy and that Jesus was that same message in human form. I may, of course, be wrong, but I am very sincerely so.

8

I Believe in the Holy Catholic Church

Okay, a show of hands: how many of you Protestants have blanched when you got to this line of the Apostles' Creed? I know I have. For a good many years I simply went silent as those words passed overhead like a suspicious-looking spy plane. It seems that so many of us have had that kind of response that the editors of the new United Methodist Hymnal saw fit to put a little asterisk after the word "catholic" in the creed. Down below you can find the reference, which merely says, "universal."

In reciting the Apostles' Creed we affirm that we believe in a "catholic" church, a universal church, a church that is big enough to include all of us, Protestant, Roman Catholic, and Orthodox alike. That is, after all, why the Roman Catholic Church bears that name. At least in the West, it was the only church for 1,500-plus years. While the church in that time was certainly not without its problems, abuses, and atrocities, it did manage (sometimes by brute force, I grant you) to hold a diversity of peoples under one theological roof.

Protestantism, on the other hand, couldn't even begin as a single entity. Luther had no sooner set up shop before there were also Calvin and Zwingli and a host of other variations on the reform theme putting out their shingles. That is, of course, a gross rendering of the Reformation, but detached observers will still note that after 2,000 years, there is still one Roman Catholic Church with basically one discernable theology (at least officially), while in a quarter of that time there have emerged too many Protestant variations to count, most of them finding it a challenge to worship under the same roof with any other. Sometimes it's impossible even for different congregations in the same denomination to find common ground.

I think that in general this fracturing of the Protestant church reflects the loss of our center. Not that the Roman Catholic Church has never strayed, but I think they have one vehicle that ensures that when they gather, their center is always before them. The Catholics have the Mass. Eucharist is why they gather.

The Communion of Saints

The broken body and shed blood of Jesus are central to every Catholic gathering. You may resent that weddings and funerals take longer because of it, but it's the tie that binds. Eucharist is the constant reminder of who and whose we are, and it is the absolute center of Catholicism. Even in days when no one understood any of the words that were spoken in the Mass, when the bell rang, the miracle occurred anyway and that man on the cross became the God on the table, available to the poorest peasant, the most miserable slave.

I don't mean to overdramatize or to uncritically say that the Catholic Church has the answer. I know the stories of those who have been deeply wounded by their exclusion from the Catholic table and other rites of the Church. We get a lot of Methodists that way. I know the picture is not always as pretty and pure as I have painted it. The Reformation and then the Counter-Reformation were sorely needed. Vatican II was a godsend, even if the sudden shift did send the folks of my generation reeling ("So, last week I was going to hell if I didn't wear a hat. Now it's okay. This church doesn't know what it's talking about. I'm outta here."). I know personally some of those deeply harmed by errant, pedophile priests.

But even with all of that, there remains something to be said for the ritual proclamation of our center at every gathering of the faithful. It doesn't particularly matter to me which theology of the Eucharist lies behind your observance. I'm not making a case for transubstantiation, consubstantiation, or anything of the kind. I'm here to argue against *insubstantiation*. Celebration of the Lord's Supper has become an insubstantial part of too many of our Protestant traditions, and I believe we are paying the price.

Celebrating the Eucharist won't ensure that no other god will creep in, but it certainly does ensure that the church always has a visible reminder of which God rightfully deserves that central place and why.

With the Protestant focus on the sermon, it's no wonder that so many of us pastors come to think of ourselves as God. The entire worship service is centered on us, with the sermon as the main event.

One thing I really took to heart in seminary (with thanks to Candler School of Theology professor Don Saliers) was the observation that the way we structure our worship—even the way we furnish our sanctuaries—is part of our proclamation. We show who is important in the relative size of the chairs in the chancel and in who gets to enter the chancel in the first place. Is there a rail that closes off the altar from "the common folk"? Can children go behind it? Whatever is central to the life of a congregation tends to be centrally located in the sanctuary. Is it the altar? The cross? The pulpit? What is the main event to which our service builds? What are the necessary elements in worship?

I led a women's retreat in my first year at the church I serve in Dover, New Hampshire. Thirty-some women gathered for a weekend to focus on the theme of worship. In one exercise, I divided them into five groups and charged each group to list five things that were critical to a worship experience: the five essential things that they would never leave out. It could be any five things, but the whole group had to agree for an item to go on the list. When they finished, we compared lists to see which items could be agreed on by all five groups. There were only two things common to all five groups: a message and singing. Some individual groups included prayer, some included Scripture. I don't recall that anybody included Communion, but maybe it received a marginal reference.

Message and music. Those are good things, but it leaves any reference to our true center solely at the discretion of the pastor and musicians. In the Mass, there is no option. Christ is proclaimed and "him crucified" every single time. Every Mass contains the story: the death, the resurrection, the hope of a banquet yet to come. It might be done without feeling. It might seem empty and rote. But even in the celebrations that seem the most void of Spirit, the broken body and shed blood are there to shout their witness from the center. Those with ears to hear, let them hear.

I realize that not all Protestant traditions have abandoned the weekly Eucharist, and I applaud those like my Episcopalian friends who have retained it. It is a brave thing to retain both word and sacrament in a culture that likes to be done with church in an hour. And I do understand the fear of other traditions that the familiarity of

a weekly observance will bring contempt or at least merely rote observance of a truly sacred act. I just believe that the benefits are worth the
risk. I have a better chance at having my cup filled if I bring it to every
single service.

Lately there is a new brand of objection from those churches who
do not want to offend the newcomer with a mysterious ritual that talks
about eating flesh and drinking blood. I am a Protestant at least in part
because I agree that weekly worship is a point of entry for the seeker as
well as a gathering of the baptized. I do want to have moments of
education and verbal proclamation, rituals that are open and acces-
sible, and liturgy that is understandable to those who are walking
through a church door for the first time. But I believe my proclamation would be compromised if the service implied that everything in
the Christian faith could be easily grasped by someone walking in cold
off the street.

I want a service that makes encounter with the living God desirable,
possible, and completely beyond my comprehension. I want grace to
be amazing, not cut and dried. I want moments of transcendence,
where even the most seasoned churchgoer will realize how little we
truly understand of what God has done for us. I want to live out, every
week, the truth that the victim we kill and consume is the Bread of Life
who in that self-giving can lead us away from our cycles of violence to
relationships of reciprocity. I want Eucharist.

The Resurrection of the Body

Restoring Eucharist to our churches is, I think, a very concrete way that
we can keep the lid off of all our various God-boxes. Who can possibly
think they have God all figured out when confronted with this strange
act? Eucharist is the square peg for our round holes, the enigma that
reminds us that no matter how much theological training we might
have, when we put the bread in our mouths and touch the wine to our
lips, we haven't got a clue. The tiniest child understands no less than we
do. It is mystery.

I am always amused when I hear parents keeping their children
from the table until such time as they can "understand what they
are doing." Which of us understands what we are doing? Eucharist
is one of those times when we don't know with our minds but with
our bodies. We cannot articulate what our body knows as it receives

nourishment; we cannot say what goes on in our soul in the moment of grace. We can only say that we have received it. We can only ring the bell and say that the miracle has happened, inviting the guests to be as astonished as the steward that the bridegroom has saved the very best wine until now. Understand what we are doing? Surely you jest.

Because we cannot understand, at least in a way that can be definitively articulated, we cannot close the box. If only for this one thing, we must leave off the lid, because we can never be sure we have understood it all. Eucharist is the consummate box-exploder. Just when you think that faith is all sheep in green pastures beside still waters, here comes an execution on a hill that looks like a skull. Just when you think that God protects the faithful and destroys the wicked, here is the flesh of God's own Son torn apart by nails. Just as we are tempted to glory in our sufferings, using them to justify ourselves and condemn our oppressors, here comes Jesus' broken body and shed blood given to save his executioners. Just when you think that death is the end of all things, here comes a born-again death bringing the offer of new life. Try to keep closing the box if you will, but I'm here to tell you your arms will get tired from opening and closing it all the time. Trust me, it's easier to leave the lid off.

And the Life Everlasting

No, I'm not going to convert to Catholicism, at least not until they allow me into the priesthood, which will probably be a while. But I do believe that Catholicism has a message for all of us as we seek ways to heal the divisions in the Body of Christ. Our brokenness can be transformed into saving grace, just as the broken Body of Christ has always done. But for that to happen, we need to offer it up. We need to remove the lid that keeps it hidden in our God-box and allow God to reach in and place it with all the others on the altar. We cannot save ourselves.

We need to get to the point where I was when I left for seminary: our God-boxes completely empty except for the certain knowledge of our calling to become the people of God. Our self-righteousness must be gone. Our notion that we completely understand all the ways of God and all the nuances of Scripture must vanish into the vastness of mystery. We must stand as I did in the Clarkston, Georgia, United Methodist church, look back over our lives, and say, "Damn. Even now

I don't have it right." (Probably we must quit writing books that say "we must.")

How do we do it? How do we keep from diminishing ourselves and others by trying to make a limitless God fit in a limited space? Restoring the centrality of the Eucharist, I believe, is one answer of many that might reflect the same theme: keep the main thing the main thing. At least that seems to be how it all hangs together in heaven. The book of Revelation gives us some startling oddities in many places. But perhaps stranger than the beasts with many horns, the colored horses, or the angels with their seals and trumpets full of wrath and misery, is the picture of unity amidst the diversity of heaven.

We have this tendency to think that heaven has just God, angels, and the souls of the saints, but Revelation gives us a much more diverse picture. We have angels, yes. But we also have twenty-four elders and four living creatures, cherubim and seraphim and "a great multitude that no one could count, from every nation, from all tribes and peoples and languages, standing before the throne and before the Lamb" (7:9). What are they doing? Doxology. They are standing around the throne, with the Main Thing in the middle, singing "Amen! Blessing and glory and wisdom and thanksgiving and honor and power and might be to our God forever and ever! Amen" (7:12).

It's the same thing back in chapter 4 and ahead in chapter 19. Handel's *Messiah* and a good bit of our hymnody would be severely compromised if we took Luther's advice and scrapped Revelation. Worship in heaven is kept from division because the focus is on the praise of God. They take the crowns from their heads, those symbols of their power and entitlement and righteousness, and throw them down before the throne (4:10–11) as they sing, "You are worthy, our Lord and God, to receive glory and honor and power, for you created all things, and by your will they existed and were created."

Notice how different our hymns are. We do sing about this scene in "Holy, Holy, Holy," but we sing about it as the experience of others: "Casting down *their* golden crowns around the glassy sea." When we put ourselves in the picture, it comes out as it does in "Mansion over the Hilltop": "I want a mansion, a harp, and a crown!" Others are there to give praise, we are there to receive our reward.

That reflects, I think, our loss of center. John's vision of heaven has it right. All attention is focused on God, and even heavenly crowns are flung away. Nothing else matters, and with all creatures of our God and King focused on their one love, all become one in and with that love. There is no division. The multitude from tribes and races that have hated and obliterated each other on earth have no room to even think about the issues that nurtured their hatreds. Their focus is elsewhere. It is where it belongs: on God.

Suppose we did that? I know it is perhaps as naive as the 1960's question, "What if they had a war and nobody came?" but still I think it bears asking. Suppose we weren't focused on each other. Suppose we gave our attention to the praise of God so completely that we had no brain cells left over to worry about whether Jesus was actually born of a virgin? Suppose we forgot to think about whether the person next to us had ever professed faith to our satisfaction? Suppose that we were so in love with God and so wrapped up in acts of adoration that we glossed over even the most heinous sins going on around us and God had to be the one to judge it all? Suppose God was so central to our worship that, standing in a circle around the throne, we could not even see each other except through the face of God?

> And so with all your people on earth and all the company of heaven, we praise your name and join in their unending hymn, "Holy, holy, holy Lord. God of power and might. Heaven and earth are full of your glory. Hosanna in the highest. Blessed is He who comes in the name of the Lord. Hosanna in the highest."

. . . and that from a former Baptist. Better keep the lid off of your box. With God all things are possible.

Sealed in the Tomb?

When Jesus first shows up on the public scene at age thirty, life is grand. He is healing the sick, casting out demons, feeding the multitudes, defying nature, and encouraging the love of God. Great stuff. People are happy. But gradually, over the three-year span of his ministry, people begin to see that this Jesus has an edge.

The religious leaders are the first to notice. They are angry because he won't abide by the religious law and is teaching thousands of people all this dangerous stuff: that doing what is right is more important than doing what is legal, that forgiveness and mercy are better than punishment, and that heretics who act with love are going to get into

God's kingdom faster than those who believe all the right things but have no works to back it up. If they let him keep it up, they'll have anarchy on their hands and their power will be gone.

The rest of the people are happy longer, but eventually they, too, are upset. They want a political savior, not a spiritual one. Israel in Jesus' day is an occupied country, and they want somebody to pull together an army to overthrow Rome. That's why they cheered as Jesus rode into Jerusalem on Palm Sunday, and his refusal to do it is why they became angry enough to kill him. The two factions come together at the end. Betrayed by one of his own disciples, Jesus is subjected to a mockery of a trial, verbal and physical abuse, and finally an execution so inhumane it was against the law to crucify a Roman citizen.

At last this trouble-making Jesus was dead. The soldiers had verified that he was dead by lancing his side with a spear, and his body had been taken down and placed in a tomb. But the Pharisees were nervous. Jesus had predicted he would rise from the dead after three days. What if his followers came and stole the body and then went around telling people he had risen? Better to see the matter through and be very sure this Jesus incident is over. So they go to Pilate and ask for a guard of soldiers to secure the tomb. They get their soldiers, they roll the stone in front of the entrance to seal Jesus inside the tomb, and post an armed watch.

It's easy for us to look back and say, "Poor little Pharisees. Didn't they know they couldn't seal up the power of God with a rock and a few guards?" But to think that way is to be blind to our own nature. The struggle between the Pharisees bent on keeping Jesus in the tomb and God bent on getting him out has been going on now for some 2,000 years, and the struggle continues today. We keep on trying to keep Jesus in the tomb, to keep the lid on the box, and God keeps letting him out.

I believe our tomb today is the church, and people both within and without have a vested interest in sealing Jesus into that tomb and keeping him there. The world outside the church, for the most part, is happy to have Jesus in the neighborhood, just so long as he stays put inside the church and doesn't go spreading any of his hare-brained ideas out and about in the community. Sit on top of that box and keep it closed.

Think about it. How would our economy survive if people stopped buying what they didn't need, or if they shared their wealth instead of hoarding it? The Great Depression was a thriving economy compared with the effect that living the economics of Jesus would have on the country. I am absolutely serious about that. Christian faith, as Jesus taught it and as the earliest Christians lived it, is a threat to every system of power.

The foundation on which our entire economy is built is greed. The countries of sub-Saharan Africa spend more each year repaying debt than on all primary education and health care. In Tanzania, where forty percent of the population dies before the age of thirty-five, the government spends nine times more on foreign debt repayment than on health care. Forgive us our debts? A Jesus that is allowed to escape from the church would mean economic collapse. Thomas Jefferson said, "Indeed I tremble for my country when I reflect that God is just." Post a guard at the doors, nail the box shut, don't let him out!

But it isn't just the world outside the church that wants to seal the tomb. At some level, we are all much more comfortable with a Jesus who will stay where we put him and do what we say. As long as we know where he is, we're fine. We'll come and visit the grave every Sunday as long as he will not follow us out and interfere with our lives Monday through Saturday.

Why, if Jesus were allowed out of the church, we wouldn't be able to live the way we want. Things might be expected of us. Instead of just praying to God to give us things or to help us from distress, we might have to be a part of our own answered prayers. Steve, a man in the Dover, New Hampshire, church, lived this out. For many months, Steve asked us to pray for his friend who would die if he did not receive a new kidney. Finally, God asked Steve to put his kidney where his mouth was. Steve became the kidney donor for his friend. God might ask us to associate with people we don't like. We might have to rescue people that we think deserve their punishment. We might have to change. For God's sake, seal the tomb! Support the church, keep it going, but just don't open the doors and let Jesus out!

Welcome to the fearful, joyous, terrible, wonderful news of Easter morning. He's escaped! Jesus, stubborn as always, refused to stay dead. More than that, he refused to stay in the tomb. Jesus doesn't rise from the dead then whip out his cell phone and call the disciples to come to the tomb for a resurrection party. He's up. He's outta there. When the women come on Easter morning, they don't witness the resurrection. It's already happened. They find the grave clothes in a heap and Jesus is gone. Where? The angels tell them he has gone ahead of them to Galilee, back about his business of spreading the good news of God's scandalous love. He's out of the box and bids us to follow.

So what does that mean? Should we demolish the tomb and forget about church? No, the tomb still has a critically important function: it's just a different function than it used to be. The proclamation of the Christian faith is that Jesus has changed the very nature of death, and therefore the nature of the tomb. It's no longer the place to seal in the dead. It is the resurrection place.

When I talk about church as the resurrection place, I'm not just referring to the life after death that we proclaim at funerals. That's part of its meaning, but not nearly all of it. What Jesus made available to us is not just eternal life after physical death, but a brand-spanking-new spiritual life here and now. We are more than the sum of our body parts, our genes, and our hormones. We have soul and spirit and an energy that allows us to connect with things beyond ourselves. When your soul or spirit reaches out and meets the world-creating, star-throwing, sea-roaring energy of God, your life will change forever, starting now and never ending. Life is so different it seems, looking back, that life before wasn't really life but death. And so we talk of spiritual rebirth, of resurrection, and it is the job of the church to provide a sacred space in the world where that can happen.

Typically we evaluate a church by the programs it has, the budget it supports, the numbers it attracts in worship, the style of the worship services. People pick a church because they like the music or the Sunday school program; they leave because the style of worship is too traditional or too contemporary or because the pastor or programs didn't meet their needs. Well, all those things are important, but they're important only insofar as they serve the function of resurrection. The sole purpose of the church is to bring the dead to life and then to send those resurrected people out in service to the world. When we plan what happens in our worship services, the *only* relevant question is, "Will it bring the dead to life?" Will worship in this way allow people to encounter the living God? All else is secondary and can come and go with the wind. This is the resurrection place.

And when it happens, when the dead are raised, they're outta here. Like Jesus, a resurrected church doesn't stay in a closed box. It goes back out into the world to tell everybody the good news that this greed-driven rat race that we are taught to live is not the only way.

There is another. The tomb has a place and a purpose, but the central proclamation of our faith is that the tomb is not where we are meant to stay. We do not come here to reverence the dead body of Jesus. We come here to give up *our* dead body and to be given a new life that is a channel of the very power of God.

As disciples of Jesus, we follow him into the tomb in death and then we follow him right back out again transformed, renewed, alive. That's the true experience of church. We come here, and if the proclamation is true, we face all that is dead about us. That's not comfortable. God forbid that the church should become the comfortable place where things always stay the same. That is completely opposed to our mission. When Jesus gets loose in a church, nothing but nothing stays the same. Ask the Pharisees. Ask the disciples just how comfortable and unchanging their lives were. If the church is being the true church, it will make us uncomfortable, and it will force us to change.

It is here that we face the news that we are dead, and we grieve, we argue with God, we rebel against the news. But finally, we admit that what we have is an empty shell. And in that moment—in the moment when we say to God, "Okay, I admit it, my life means nothing and is going nowhere except round and round on an ever-faster hamster wheel"—in the moment when we say with both heart and mouth, "Take this shell, God, and do with it as you will"—the earth shakes, the stone is rolled away, and running out to tell the good news, we are alive as never before. He is risen! I am risen! You can be, too!

That's all there is to say on Easter, or on any day really. It's all I care about. My prayer for the church is that it be the resurrection place. I want every person who encounters the church to have the opportunity to meet the God who has given me the only life worth living. Because in the moment of that meeting, the breath of God will blow into your lungs a life like you have never known. Whether we shout and dance or kneel and pray, whether we sing or chant or swing from the balcony makes not the first bit of difference. The only thing that matters in the world is that you come to know and love the God who made you. The God who came to earth as a man named Jesus. The God who conquered death so that our tomb could be the beginning rather than the end.

It's a very strange message, to be sure. But across two thousand years of concerted effort to seal the tomb and guard the door, it has not only endured, but has spread to all the world. Do you need to live again?

Have you been sealed in the tomb of a pointless life? Look up and meet the God of life. This is the resurrection place. Come inside. Wrap up your old life in grave clothes, give it to God, and then watch the door to your tomb open to a bright new dawn. He is risen. The lid is blown off the hinges. My apologies to those who would like it otherwise, but Jesus is on the loose. He is risen and has gone on ahead of us to Galilee. Well, what are you waiting for?